Living and Cooking Vietnamese

Living and Cooking
Vietnamese

By Paula Tran

CORONA PUBLISHING CO.
SAN ANTONIO 1990

Copyright © 1990 by Paula Patillo Tran

No part of this book may be reproduced by any mechanical, photographic, or electronic process, nor otherwise transmitted or copied for public or private use, except for purposes of review, without the written permission of the publisher.

Corona Publishing Company
1037 South Alamo
San Antonio, Texas 78210

Design by Kathleen Giencke
Illustrations by Lyn Belisle

Library of Congress Catalog Card No. 89-82342
ISBN 0-931722-79-9

Manufactured in the United States of America

For Ha . . .

    the peace of the River

    (1962 — 1989)

ACKNOWLEDGEMENTS

David Bowen, who nurtured and finally published this volume, once told me, "Publishing a book is similar to giving birth to a baby." In many ways his analogy is appropriate: from inception to delivery the project monopolizes one's life; the "labor pains" can be long and arduous; yet the creation represents a union of body and spirit. And like the mother in the birth process, the writer of a book, while central to the outcome, relies on the wisdom and the kindness of many others.

First, I want to thank my parents, James and Billie Patillo. Mom has always been my personal critic, loving enough to be tactful, yet honest enough to point out my deficiencies. Dad, on the other hand, doesn't think I *have* any deficiencies, an attitude that has bound me to the pursuit of success. To these fine people go my love, my respect, my gratitude.

My "second" set of parents, Ba and No Tran, came to me through my marriage to their son. An integral part of my life, they too are deserving of my appreciation. Ba, a paradox of gruffness and gentleness, has claimed me as daughter, an honor I hope to prove worthy of. Without Ma, however, there could be no *Living and Cooking Vietnamese*, for these recipes are hers, a product of her native country and traditions which must be preserved.

I have also profited from invaluable moral and practical support from many colleagues, scholars I am fortunate enough to call "friends." Carol Ann Britt, Susan Rodriguez, and Mary Rauch contributed valuable suggestions and encouragement. Another reader, Barbara Stanush, has opened her heart and life to my work, as well as to this amazing culture. To this gracious, talented lady I extend my thanks.

Al Wesolowsky, editor of the *Journal of Field Archaeology*, has offered more than just the prodigious amount of time he spent so carefully revising my manuscript. He has provided wit, humor, a tightness that I could never have managed without his technical expertise. His friendship and encouragement I will always value.

Additionally, thanks to Joyce Hibbs for her patience in taking the cover picture of our family. How calm she was each time she suggested, "I do believe the photographs would be better if Jonathan were to keep his tongue in his mouth!"

To my very special friend, Elisa Gonzalez, I cannot thank her enough for her unqualified support, her sense of humor, and her unfailing loyalty. Elisa's beauty of spirit has given my life an added dimension.

Certainly, no acknowledgements page would be complete without a reference to my children: Sunni, Jason, and Jonathan, my most precious gifts from God. And finally, my beloved Lac, who knows me better than I know myself. This complex, intense man resembles a Chinese Box, a contraption composed of many layers which are difficult to discern. Throughout the years, Lac has opened many of these "layers", to me, some of which I share in this text. I eagerly await others. I thank him for walking this path with me; he has wrapped me in rainbows.

CONTENTS

INTRODUCTION

When I first began this project—seemingly eons ago—I envisioned a very different product than the one you are now reading. I had wanted to compile my mother-in-law's recipes, as a tribute to the gentle woman who had so patiently taught me to cook Vietnamese-style. If nothing else came of our many hours of translation and transcription, the recipes would at least be preserved for my children, who must learn to value two very different traditions.

As work progressed, however, I realized that I was involved in much more than a collection of recipes. Food and family are so central to Vietnamese life that what emerged was a memoir of my wonderful marriage and an introduction to a mysterious, proud people whose four-thousand-year-old culture centers on devotion to family, loyalty to friends, and courtesy to strangers.

There is a Vietnamese maxim that "The first pleasure in the world is eating." Having been part of a Vietnamese family for over ten years, I can attest to its validity among these new immigrants to our land. Ma, my mother-in-law, may well spend as much time arranging her foods on the platters for the most attractive display as she does preparing them. A major concern is for textures; a Vietnamese cook will blend crisp lettuce leaves or other raw vegetables with thin meat slices or she may stir-fry beef, pork, and seafood in one dish.

What one doesn't find is the European-American division of foods into successive courses: appetizer/soup/salad/entree/dessert. Vietnamese meals (which are usually long social events) are not served according to any prescribed sequence of courses. Rather, a Vietnamese meal may be described s a series of surprises. Soups, as you see in Chapter IV, are a staple and may turn up at breakfast or as the centerpiece of an evening meal. So this book is Vietnamese in its organization as well as its content. Groups of recipes follow each chapter of text; within each group, recipes are ranged in order of increasing complexity. An index at the back will help you locate recipes according to more familiar categories.

The location of Vietnam on the Southeast Asian peninsula accounts for much of the country's culinary identity, as well as its political and historical identity. This tiny agricultural nation has absorbed Chinese, French, and American influences, though not to the extent that most anthropologists would expect of a country under continual domination for centuries.

Since Vietnam was ruled by China for approximately 1000 years, Chinese influences on the culture must be expected. Chief among them were their governmental institutions and administration and an elaborate dike system to improve the irrigation process. (Eventually the Vietnamese became known as the Dutch of the Far East for their extensive dike-building.)

Despite the long period of control by China, gastronomic historians express surprise at how minor the Chinese influence has been on Vietnamese cooking. The Vietnamese learned to cook with a wok and to use chopsticks from its northern neighbor, but essentially the comparison ends there. Perhaps a good analogy would be the relationship between the United States and its neighbor Mexico. Gourmets can find fine Mexican food anywhere in the Southwest, but the farther north one travels, the lesser the Mexican influence. So too in Vietnam, the farther south one travels, the lesser the Chinese influence on the food.

Indeed, the two cuisines are remarkably different. For example, lamb is a common dish in Chinese cooking, but not in Vietnamese. Conversely, shallots and lemongrass occur in the Vietnamese diet, but not in the Chinese. The Chinese people prefer to stir-fry their main dishes, whereas the "people of the South" chose to simmer or barbeque theirs. Vietnamese food is very rarely prepared with alcohol, while many Chinese recipes call for rice wine.

The fresh, clean taste of Vietnamese cooking derives from the generous use of fresh herbs and seasonings: garlic, lemongrass, chili peppers, mint, scallions, cilantro, lemon and lime. Raw or lightly steamed vegetables and fruit are frequent ingredients. Because foods are never prepared in animal fat nor served with sugary sauces common in Chinese cuisine, the Vietnamese diet is wholesome and nutritious as well.

A major difference between the two cuisines is the absence of soy sauce in Vietnamese cooking. *Nuoc mam*, often called "fish sauce," is the nearest equivalent. Without this staple in the kitchen, there is no possibility of genuine Vietnamese cooking. (For more details on this and other interesting ingredients, please check the Glossary.)

Food is so important to the Viets that one of their major concerns as the refugees landed on our shores was that they would not be able to eat properly. Where will they find the *bidau*, a squash that grows to four feet length; or the *bau*, a squash the size of a large watermelon? Will they be able to find *dau bap*? (Yes, it is our familiar okra.) These foods are now becoming common here, as women like my mother-in-law plant and grow their own little touch of home. At the same time, they are introducing their American friends to a new, exciting way to eat.

Vietnamese-style!

I
Dojo Princess

"Calm yourself, child," Mom soothed. "They'll be here soon. Unless, of course, Lac's decided to return to Vietnam." I couldn't even fake a response to my mother's half-hearted jest. I was beyond impatience with waiting. Lac was almost an hour late, and on our wedding day!

Twisting on my finger the ring that Lac would soon wear, I reminded my mother, "Oh, but we're all on time, Mom. Vietnam time. When Lac says 6:00, he *means* 7:30." I studied the simple ring of black jade edged in gold, engraved with my name. Lac's original design was in stark contrast to the flashy diamond-and-gold wedding sets most of my friends cherished. We had had a difficult time finding a jeweler who could fashion our matched pair but Lac refused to accept anything less, or anything more, than the simplicity of this joining of jet and gold.

What if he *had* changed his mind? What if he finally recognized the clash of cultures that our marriage would surely produce? Perhaps at the last moment his parents had succeeded in convincing him that a young Vietnamese beauty would be a more appropriate bride than this outspoken American divorcee who was blissfully ignorant of *chung toc doc nhat* — the "superior race." These thoughts clanged about in my mind as I wandered from den to kitchen to living room and back again, like an irresolute pin-ball.

As more minutes dragged by, I was by now concluding that I had made a major mistake by agreeing to a traditional Buddhist wedding. I had done it in order to placate Lac's parents. But they had been so vociferous in their displeasure when Lac had announced our engagement some three months earlier! Lac had tried to spare my feelings. "Well, yes, they *were* a little upset when I told them. We just won't invite them to the wedding."

"Lac, we *have* to invite them!" All my Italian ancestry recoiled at the thought of deliberately slighting parents—even old-world parents who feared the disruption of familial harmony by this foreign intruder. "Wait a second," I recalled saying to myself then. "Just who *is* the foreigner here?" It was I who had walked into his world, not the other way around . . .

As a recent divorcee in San Antonio, Texas, I had begun karate lessons several months prior to meeting Lac. It was long enough to contract the dreaded "dojo princess" syndrome, a malady that often afflicts females in this male-dominated sport. One night, as usual, I entered the office to greet and bow to the instructor. He sat at his desk, puffing on asphyxiating Korean cigarettes and talking quietly with a youngster, whom I assumed to be a new class member. Smiling, I directed my attention toward him—or was it her? Shoulder-length hair, dimpled baby face, and untied *gi* (karate uniform) offered no concrete clues to the sex of this newcomer. Not even the instructor's introduction settled the matter, for the name come out one long, indecipherable word. "This is Chranvanlock."

"Hi." I acknowledged the one-sided introduction, then remembering the cultural taboo, quickly brushed aside the temptation to pat the Oriental Cabbage Patch Kid's head.

A shy half-grin was my only response. "No matter," I thought. "I'll befriend this little novice, help him get the feel of dojo life. Perhaps tonight I could work privately with him, introduce the first form. We dojo princesses must surely honor our *noblesse oblige*." I fairly bubbled over with the milk of human kindness.

Bowing, I left the office to enter the dojo. After greeting my classmates, I set about warming up on the mats. A hundred jumping jacks . . . fifty sit-ups . . . twenty-five push-ups . . . I was so absorbed in my stretching that for a while I missed the undercurrent that rippled through the large gym. "He's here!" I overheard a senior brown belt exclaim. "Tonight!"

"Who?" I grunted, from the full extension of a hurdle stretch.

"The Grand Master from Vietnam. Former Southeast Asian Champion. Teaching tonight! Hot stuff happening!" The room buzzed with excitement.

My interest was mildly piqued, for the closest I had come to a grand master was a picture of O Sensei, an elderly, bearded Japanese who had originated the art of Aikido, a beautiful non-aggressive style. I imagined myself sitting at the feet of so revered a teacher, serving him tea as he inspired us with cryptic Oriental sayings which I would pretend to understand.

This foray into fantasy land was broken as the door swung open, and the clamor suddenly fell silent. All eyes riveted on the entrance. Briefly, nothing. Then he appeared. The Grand Master paused, surveyed the group—was that disgust I read in his eyes?—then strode into the room, resolutely tying his *gi* with the wide black belt, symbol of a master.

The transformed Oriental doll—the youngster I had planned to introduce to dojo experience — signaled the senior student to prepare us for bowing in. Within minutes all the students in the room knew they were indeed in the presence of an extraordinary force. And they all attempted to impress him, if not with their skill, then with their determination. Me included — no, me especially. I had to atone for my blunder somehow.

I kicked higher than I had ever kicked, punched harder than I had ever punched, and *kiaied* (karate scream) louder than I ever wish to again. I caught him watching me out of the corner of his eye. Was he impressed? Could he actually like what he was seeing? Did he recognize 110% effort when he saw it?

He started toward me, threading a path among the students. As he passed me, without breaking stride, without acknowledging me, he whispered, "You're doing it wrong." The first words of the man I had by then determined to marry.

For three years thereafter I studied with Mr. Lac (as we all called him) and constantly laid traps designed to move our relationship from professional to personal. For three years he managed to sidestep those traps with Oriental delicacy and efficiency. He did, however, turn over the financial reins of the dojo to me, for he has never wished to be bothered with so mundane a responsibility. Had I known him better, I would have recognized the significance of the trust he had placed in me. As it was, I was simply delighted that I had more reason to talk with him, though he never was one to converse freely with anyone.

About six months after our first meeting, Lac invited me to dinner at his home—a major breakthrough. After changing clothes five times and redoing my hair that had just been styled, I set out, determined to impress his family. Little did I know what that would entail. Several Americans were there, including the Shackelfords, who had sponsored Lac's family out of the refugee camp. Delightful people, Al and Frances befriended me and spent the evening making polite conversation. I follwed their lead, for I knew nothing of civilized behavior in Vietnamese households. When they rose to leave, I too stood up, bowed, and began my profuse thanks. "No," Lac declared flatly. "The real meal is just starting. You must stay to sample our food."

Sample our food? What did he think I had just done? Having found the flavors strange but mouth-watering, I had gorged to the point of humiliation, I thought. My confusion must have registered clearly on my face, for Ha, Lac's younger sister, laughed and said, "Oh yes. Feasting will go on for hours. You must not leave now."

I stayed but felt totally out of place. The change in atmosphere when all the Americans left was almost palpable. Conversation among the family and guests reverted to Vietnamese only, and they swirled about me like swarms of bumblebees. The women gathered in the kitchen to prepare the "second" serving, while the men huddled in corners, smoking and gossiping. Sitting alone at the table, I searched my repertoire of communication skills, then realized that two semesters of conversational French provided scant avenue for cultural exchange here. Finally Ha, bless her, recognized my sense of isolation and joined me.

Soon the women began spreading the main feast, most of which I could not identify. No longer were we served on fine china plates with silverware. Before me appeared a small rice bowl and chopsticks, (which Ha tactfully exchanged for a fork). Nodding and nibbling and constantly grinning, but fooling no one, I tried not to embarrass Lac before his friends and relatives. It would be many years before I could read any emotion in Lac's impassive face; had I been more perceptive I would have realized that he shared the tension I felt.

By May, three years after our first meeting, I had planned a small party and of course invited Lac to attend. Since he had always accepted my invitations and never came, I was stunned when he arrived with the Kong brothers, Allen and Wah. He stayed long after all the other guests had left, filling me in on the gaps in the tapestry of his life. On his role in the war, on his capture and imprisonment. On his sentence of execution and the daring escape, during which he was shot in the back. As if his dam of silence had burst, he flooded me with his past.

Then with dawn approaching, he shyly kissed me and left. From that day on he visited my apartment daily. Two weeks later, eager to demonstrate my domestic talents, I prepared dinner for him. After a heavy meal of lasagna, garlic loaves, and red wine—which on our honeymoon he admitted to hating!—we settled on the couch to watch a grade-B thriller, all our joint finances would support. At some point during the movie, he said, so quietly that I had to strain to hear him, "So. When are we going to get married?"

"What? Are you serious? Married?"

Since he offered nothing else but sat quietly watching me, I added, "When do you want to get married?"

"How about next month?"

"June? That's only a week away. But I guess it's possible."

Then, despite the late hour, I raced to the phone and dialed my sister Sharron's number. "Sharron! Sharron!" I exclaimed to her groggy greeting. "Guess what! Lac and I are getting married. And I want you to be in the wedding."

"That's great," she replied. "Who is this?"

By the next afternoon we both realized that two weeks was just not long enough to prepare our families, let alone plan a wedding. August, we agreed would be better for everyone. First the families. Lac's, we anticipated, would prove more formidable, for every Vietnamese mother this side of the Rio Grande had been trying to tie him to her daughter. My parents, on the contrary just wanted me to find *anyone* who would treat me well.

On the day Lac chose to inform his parents, Wah accompanied him. An hour, two hours passed before they returned. "How did it go, honey?"

"Oh, just fine," he lied. "Everything went well."

"Well?" Wah hooted, as he threw himself across the couch. "You should have seen him, Paula. He was a crazy man. *No one's* ever seen Lac like that!"

So much for diplomacy.

After the Tran clan reaction we decided that a joint attack on my parents might be preferable to my running the play alone. We invited ourselves to dinner; then when everyone was settled in the den for the after-dinner ritual of *Jeopardy*, we announced our plans. For a moment the silence frightened me. "Oh, no, please don't say anything to humiliate me," I prayed. As if in response to that prayer, Mom said, "Paula, that's wonderful! If you're sure that's what you want." Dad merely stared at us and said nothing. Finally, he reached over to shake Lac's hand, as close to a blessing as Dad could give.

Because of limited finances, we planned a simple wedding at the Japanese Sunken Gardens. We selected invitations of rose and pink, and Lac lettered our names in delicate Chinese characters. They were in the mail by the second week in July for an August 18 ceremony. Immediately thereafter, Ma and Ba called to launch plans of their own. First they had to ask for my hand formally, one of many traditions I would come to honor.

Again we all met in the family den. Ba and Dad drank to each other's health, after which Ba made a long speech concerning the role of the family in Vietnamese society. He concluded with the request for my hand. Dad simply stared blankly at him, until he repeated the request.

"Oh!" Dad said. "She's been doing exactly as she pleases for many years. I can't start telling her what to do now. If she wants to marry your son, I'm certain she will." Not quite the answer Ba had anticipated. Nonetheless, he proceeded with attempts to revise the plans we had so carefully laid out. Soon it became obvious that Ba visualized an entirely different ceremony than we had planned, a Buddhist extravaganza. Mom and Dad approved out intimate garden wedding with early evening reception. Just cake, punch, open bar, finger sandwiches, mints, and nuts. Ba and Ma feared the disgrace of so shabby a party. At that point neither set of parents could accept or comprehend the other's viewpoints, so to satisfy both, we compromised: A Buddhist ceremony for the Vietnamese community, a Christian wedding (performed by a black belt licensed minister from Lac's dojo) for my parents.

And double the pressure on Lac and me.

CHOPSTICK ETIQUETTE

My first major lesson in "becoming Oriental" involved learning to master the *doi dua,* or chopsticks. As in all other Oriental cultures, chopsticks serve as "silverware" for the Vietnamese. Even the Westernized children of Vietnamese immigrants generally prefer them to forks and spoons.

Despite the protests of many frustrated non-Orientals, chopsticks can be used more efficiently than silverware. In fact, the word itself derives from a Cantonese dialect and means "the quick stick."

The Vietnamese prove most creative in their uses for the chopsticks. As well as eating utensils, they are used as tongs to cook with, as skewers for meats, as ornaments for a woman's hair, and even as a weapon in certain Kung-Fu styles.

According to Vietnamese tradition, it is bad luck to eat with a pair of mismatched chopsticks.

Passing food from one person to another using chopsticks indicates a serious conflict or breach will develop between the two. Custom dictates that one person serving another must place the food in the bowl before the other may pick it up with chopsticks.

Customarily a Vietnamese will never ask for chopsticks if they are not served. They find the American habit of requesting them in an Oriental restaurant both amusing and ostentatious.

When a Vietnamese person places the chopsticks on the table for visitors, a gentle tapping on the table to level them indicates respect.

If a Vietnamese inadvertently brings out an extra pair of chopsticks, this indicates that unexpected company will arrive soon.

The Vietnamese believe that it is very bad luck to lay chopsticks so that they are crossed.

New chopsticks must be provided for every new beginning—at weddings, during the Tet, or New Year, in the "thoi noi," or leaving the cradle ceremony for babies.

The Vietnamese commonly serve their foods on large, ornate platters. Using their own chopsticks, the guests select their servings, often picking up and inspecting pieces, then laying them down and inspecting another. In very formal dining, the guest may turn over the chopsticks and use the other end for food selection.

The Vietnamese meal is much more a social encounter than it is in the United States. Even a simple family meal may take as much as an hour—several when guests are present. Speaking rapidly in a monosyllabic language, the Vietnamese commonly punctuate their conversations with elaborate gestures using their chopsticks.

Chopsticks made of wood may be purchased for as little as a dime; however, a pair of hand-carved ivory chopsticks may cost several hundred dollars.

SUGGESTIONS FOR SUCCESSFUL USE OF CHOPSTICKS:

1. Consider them to be extensions of your fingers.

2. Hold them lightly; the tighter the grip, the more likely the slip.

3. To learn to manipulate the chopsticks, practice on cotton balls or large paper wads. When you have mastered these objects, move on to large chunks of food such as dinner rolls or french fries. Eat several meals with just your family before experimenting in public.

4. Above all, relax. If you remain calm, you will manage the chopsticks more efficiently.

5. Until you become very proficient, avoid using the plastic varieties. The wooden ones are a great deal more manageable for novices.

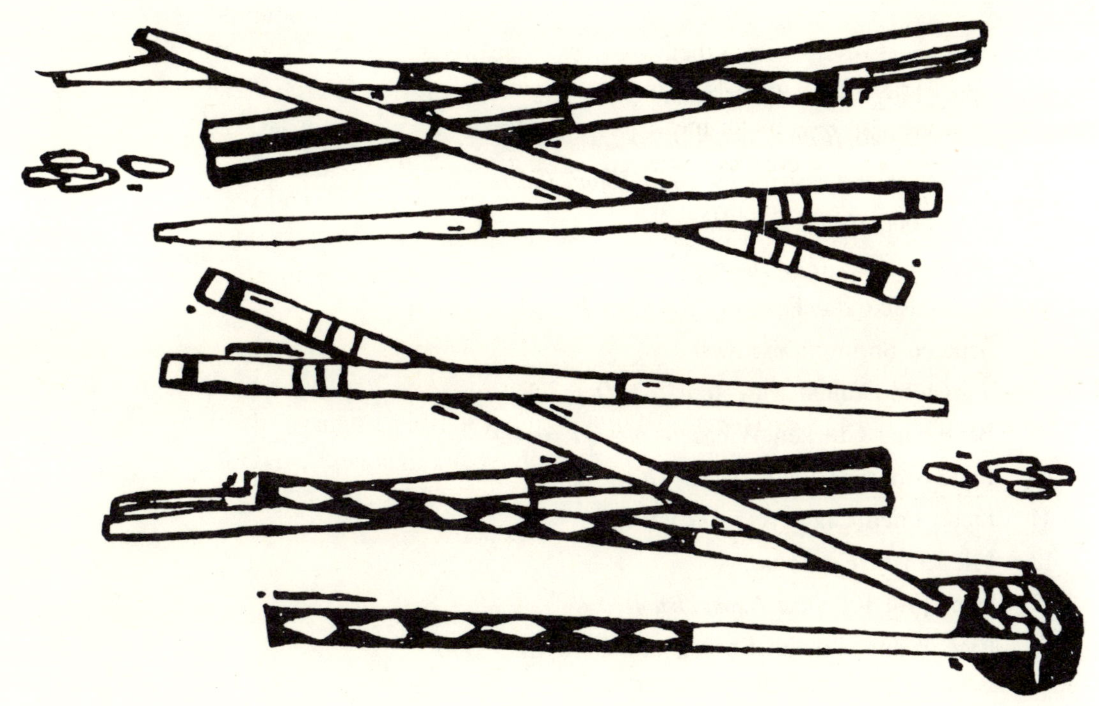

A Few Simple Dishes

1. Spicy Fish Sauce *(Nuoc Mam)*

2. Carrot Salad *(Carot Ngam Dam)*

3. Crabmeat and Asparagus Soup *(Canh Cua)*

4. Tofu Soup *(Canh Dau Hu)*

5. Wonton Soup *(Pho Hoanh Thanh)*

6. Sweet Rice and Peanuts *(Xoi Dau Phong)*

7. Sauteed Shrimp *(Tom Kho)*

8. Tomatoes Stuffed with Tofu *(Ca Don Tau Hu)*

9. Barbequed Chicken Wings *(Canh Ga Nuong)*

10. Fried Wonton *(Banh Hoanh Thanh Chien)*

11. Deep Fried Crab *(Cua Lang Bot)*

12. Fried Fish *(Ca Chien)*

13. Mint Fish Rolls *(Ca Nuong Truoi)*

14. Rice Vermicelli with Shrimp and Pork *(Bun Goi)*

Nuoc Mam
(Spicy Fish Sauce)

  2 red (serrano) chili peppers, minced
  4 garlic cloves, pressed
  3 tsp. sugar
  ½ cup Vietnamese fish sauce
1½ Tbs. lime juice, to taste
  1 cup of water

Mash the peppers, garlic, and sugar into a paste. Add the fish sauce, lime juice and water. Blend well. Seal and refrigerate.

Yield: Approximately 1½ cups.

Carot Ngam Dam
(Carrot Salad)

6 carrots, peeled
3 cups water
6 tsp. vinegar
½ tsp. salt
5 tsp. sugar

With a vegetable peeler, slice long pieces of carrot (or use a food processor if available). Roll these pieces, then cut them into tiny strips, as you would slice noodles. Combine the water, vinegar, salt, and sugar, and stir the thin carrot strips into the mixture. Marinate at least 12 hours. To serve, drain and discard the liquid.

Note: This carrot salad is always added to the spicy fish sauce when it is served with spring rolls.

Serves: 4.

Canh Cua
(Crabmeat and Asparagus Soup)

½ lb. crab meat (more if preferred)
1 16-oz. can asparagus (green/yellow)
1 16-oz. can chicken broth
2 eggs, beaten
1 tsp. cornstarch
1 tsp. MSG
1 tsp. salt (to taste)
3-4 chopped green onions
    pepper (to taste)

Put chicken broth into large saucepan. Add 2½ cans (40 oz.) water. Cook over medium heat for 15 minutes. Add crab and asparagus and bring to a boil, 10 minutes. Stir in seasonings. Then mix cornstarch with 1-3 Tbs. water. Dissolve well. Stirring vigorously, pour into soup. Continuing to stir, add the beaten eggs. Take soup off burner and add chopped green onions and pepper to taste.

Note: Although we Americans opt for convenience—and Lord knows I am more American than most—the Vietnamese would never consider using canned or fake crabmeat in any of their recipes.

Serves: 4-6.

Canh Dau Hu
(Tofu Soup)

1	package hard tofu, cut into bite-sized cubes
1	cup vegetable oil
3	green onions, minced
1	medium onion, thinly sliced
1	cup green beans, snapped into 1½-2 inch pieces
10-15	water chestnuts, thinly sliced
1	cup soy bean sauce
1	tsp. black pepper
½	gallon water
¼	lb. lean pork, thinly sliced
1½	tsp. MSG

Pour oil in wok or saucepan over high heat. Deep-fry tofu cubes until golden-brown. Drain. Next, boil water, pork, green beans, water chestnuts, onion, and soy bean sauce for 15-20 minutes. Add MSG and stir the mixture well. Add fried tofu to the soup and continue to cook for 5 more minutes. To serve: ladle soup into bowl, season with black pepper and green onion to taste.

Serves: 6-8.

Pho Hoanh Thanh
(Wonton Soup)

WONTONS
    ½ lb. ground pork
    1 small onion, finely chopped
    1 tsp. salt
    ½ tsp. pepper
    1 package wonton wrappers

SOUP
    1 16-oz. can chicken broth—or pork broth if
       preferred
    1 Tbs. preserved cabbage
    ½ tsp. MSG
    1 tsp. salt
    1 Tbs. sesame oil

Mix the chicken broth with 3 cans of water in a large saucepan. Add seasonings and simmer while you prepare the wontons. Mix all the ingredients and knead until smooth. Drop small amounts, about ½ tsp., onto the separated wonton wrappers. Fold them over into triangles or bunch all four corners up into a flower effect. You will have 30-40 little dumplings. Steam them for 10 minutes. To serve: divide wontons and place them in 4-6 soup bowls. Quickly stir sesame oil into the simmering soup and ladle over the wontons.

Serves: 4-6.

Xoi Dau Phong
(Sweet Rice and Peanuts)

   1 cup sweet rice
   ½ cup raw peanuts

Cover the rice with water and allow to soak for 1-2 hours. Then drain the water. Mix the peanuts and sweet rice, and place the mixture in a steamer. Steam for 30-40 minutes.

Note: This dish may be served with chicken or roast pork. Or it may be eaten, as Vietnamese farmers often do, with sugar. It was said that if a man ate a bowl of this sweet rice in the morning, he could work in the field all day.

Serves: 4.

Tom Kho
(Sauteed Shrimp)

       1 lb. large shrimp
       1 small onion, thinly sliced
       1 tsp. salt
       ½ cup soy sauce
       ½ tsp. MSG
       2 Tbs. cooking oil

Wash shrimp but do not remove heads or shells. Heat oil in a large skillet or wok. Lightly saute the onion, then add the shrimp. Stir constantly for 2-3 minutes. Then add salt, soy sauce and MSG. Cook another 3 minutes. Serve over rice or with French bread.

Serves: 4.

Ca Don Tau Hu
(Tomatoes Stuffed with Tofu)

6 medium tomatoes
8 oz. of tofu, preferably hard type
4 oz. of mushrooms, cleaned and finely chopped
2 green onions, finely chopped
2 tsp. fish sauce
½ tsp. pepper, or to taste
3 Tbs. cooking oil

Clean the tomatoes. Cut off the tops and core the tomatoes. Mash tofu into a paste, and mix with mushrooms, onions, and seasonings. Spoon mixture into the tomatoes. Heat oil in a skillet over a high heat. Place tomatoes, stuffed sides down, into oil. Lower heat to medium, cover the skillet. Cook for 3-4 minutes, then turn over and cook the other side for another 3-4 minutes. Ready to serve.

Serves: 6.

Canh Ga Nuong
(Barbequed Chicken Wings)

     6 chicken wings
     1 tsp. honey
     ¼ cup soy sauce
     1 tsp. hoisin sauce
     ⅛ tsp. MSG (optional)
     1 tsp. cilantro or Chinese parsley, chopped
     1 clove garlic

Mash the garlic into a paste, using a mortar and pestle, if available. (If not, mash with the flat side of a cleaver or large butcher knife.) Add the honey, soy sauce, hoisin sauce, MSG, and parsley, and stir for 1-2 minutes. Drop in the chicken wings, coat well. Cover the container and refrigerate for 1-2 hours. BBQ the chicken wings on a charcoal grill over medium heat for 10-15 minutes. Each time you turn the wings, baste them with the remaining mixture.

Note: I recognize that these wings are not barbequed Texas-style; however, the Vietnamese term "nuong" itself means "barbeque."

Yield: 6.

Banh Hoanh Thanh Chien
(Fried Wonton)

½ lb. lean ground pork
1 tsp. salt
½ tsp. pepper
½ tsp. MSG (optional)
1 egg, slightly beaten
2 dried black mushrooms
1 package of wonton wrappers

Soak mushrooms in water for 10 minutes; chop them into very tiny pieces. Then mix with the pork, seasonings, and egg. Blend well. Prepare the wontons by dropping approximately 1 tsp. of pork mixture onto the wonton square. Fold over the mixture diagonally, forming a triangle. Seal the edges and deep-fry for 3-4 minutes or until the wonton is golden brown. Serve with fish sauce (see p. 9), or sweet and sour sauce.

Note: My guests are always delighted when I serve these as appetizers. Obviously they don't realize how quick and easy wonton is to prepare. No need to share that secret, is there?

Yield: 30-40 dumplings.

Cua Lang Bot
(Deep Fried Crab)

      1 cup flour
      3 cups water
      1 egg, beaten slightly
      2 green onions, chopped fine
      1 lb. of cleaned crab meat
    1-3 cups cooking oil

Mix the flour, water, egg, and green onions in a mixing bowl. Blend until the mixture is smooth. Cut the crab meat into bite-sized pieces and place in the batter. Allow to stand 3-4 minutes, while the oil is heating in a large pot or wok. Deep-fry the coated crab pieces until golden brown, approximately 3 minutes.

Note: You can add mushrooms, onion rings, potato wedges, or okra pieces to the batter for more variety.

Serves: 3-4.

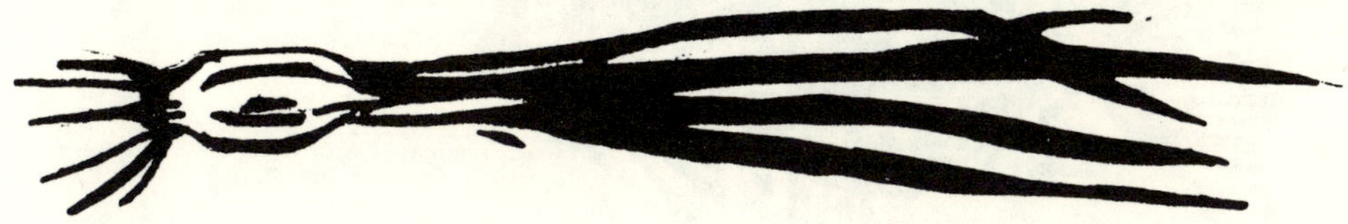

Ca Chien
(Fried Fish)

1 large redfish
1 Tbs. cooking oil
1 clove garlic

Clean fish. Pour oil in a skillet and heat over medium high flame. Crush garlic and saute lightly in skillet. Put whole fish into the pan and fry each side for approximately 5 minutes, until brown. Serve with *nuoc mam* (see p. 9), or Ginger Fish Sauce (see p. 45).

Note: Fillets will work in this recipe and will provide a quick, delicious meal for those evenings when you just don't feel like dealing with whole fish.

Serves: 2.

Ca Nuong Truoi
(Mint Fish Rolls)

1 large catfish, whole or filleted
1 small bunch of fresh mint leaves
1 package of clear (edible) rice paper
1 cup vermicelli rice noodles, cooked and drained
1 cucumber, sliced into long thin pieces
1 cup fish sauce (page 9)
½ cup peanuts, crushed

Clean the fish, then place on a barbeque grill over a hot flame. When it is fully cooked, prepare the rice paper by quickly dipping it in water. Let this sit for a minute or two, while you cut the meat off the catfish or chop the fillets. Next place meat shreds, mint leaves, noodles, and cucumber onto the rice paper and sprinkle a few peanuts over the entire mixture. Then roll the paper as you would roll an eggroll. Dip in fish sauce and enjoy!

Note: If you're wondering how to handle Vietnamese noodles, simply prepare them ahead of time, drain in a colander, and let stand until ready to use in this recipe. They may be eaten hot or cold.

Yield: Approx. 12.

Bun Goi
(Rice Vermicelli with Shrimp and Pork)

>   4 lean pork chops
>   ½ lb. shrimp, deveined and boiled
>   1 16-oz. package of rice vermicelli
>   ½ small cucumber, cut in thin slices
>   1 tsp. crushed cilantro
> 1-3 Tsp. fish sauce (page 9)

Grill and slice chops into very narrow, thin strips ("left-overs" work perfectly well in this dish!) Bring approximately ½ gallon of water to a hard boil in a large sauce pan. Stir in the vermicelli. Cook until just tender and drain in colander. Divide into four large soup bowls. Place pork slivers and shrimp pieces on top of vermicelli in each bowl. Add cucumber pieces and cilantro, to taste. Ready to serve. This dish, spiced with fish sauce, may be covered and stored in the refrigerator for later serving.

Note: This is one of my very favorite treats. Eaten either hot, lukewarm or cold, it may be prepared early in the day for later meals.

Serves: 3-4.

II
A Wedding of Two Worlds

By the time we were composing the guest list, Ba, Lac's father, proclaimed in his best English, "We not know you get married. Now no time to make big party." Ba's English may not have been his strong suit; it was (and is) nearly as monosyllabic as the Vietnamese language. But I never knew a soul who had difficulty understanding him. A typhoon doesn't speak English at all — but when it talks, everyone understands perfectly. I think Ba and a typhoon would get along nicely. Ma, his wife, had even less English, and even greater fluency in communication.

Within a month they had printed elaborate invitations of red and gold for a guest list of some 200 friends. They had ordered rich satin material from Houston for my *ao dai* or ceremonial wedding gown, measured my head for the *khan dong*, a golden crown worn by Vietnamese brides, purchased a diamond heart-shaped necklace for my engagement gift, and

arranged a full Oriental dinner for their eldest son's wedding. All on "short" notice. I have no doubts that if they had another two weeks, elephants and sampans would have been added to the ceremony.

And now I was waiting in my parents' home. It would have been inappropriate, I learned, for a young woman in the culture I was adopting to be living alone in her own apartment.

Then, with shocking suddenness, the procession arrived. Eight cars decked out with flowers, colorful streamers, and indecipherable signs. And what did these signs say anyway? For all I knew, they could have been blessings for a first-born, a prayer for a low-interest mortgage, or recipes for chicken lemongrass.

My parents greeted Lac's parents and guests, offered them a drink, then waited for their cues. Had my family been Vietnamese Buddhists, we would have all offered tribute, prayers, and sacrifice to our ancestors before the family altar. Our guests had to settle for a drink.

After that brief ceremony my parents would have traditionally presented gifts to the groom's family, including a whole roasted pig. Historically, that pig served another purpose than just nourishment: if the bride were found not to be virgin, the offended groom's family sent the ears back to the bride's family, a sign of total disgrace and utter loss of face. Fortunately I remained ignorant of this custom for many years after our wedding. Since I was a divorcee, perhaps my family would have received the tail, as well.

In any case, no pig was offered to my fiance and his family. Ba and Ma, however, brought four enormous baskets full of fruit as presents for my parents. These, according to tradition, were to be passed out among friends and relatives after the wedding, a demonstration of Oriental largesse. Mom, thinking it would be churlish to give away such sumptuous gifts, probably canned them as preserves.

Drinks downed and fruit accepted, we were ready to leave. Very carefully, Ba counted the bridal party, determining that only an even number be seated in each car. It is very bad luck for an odd number to be associated with a Vietnamese wedding: such a lamentable oversight guarantees trouble between the bride and groom.

Mack Sennett and his Keystone Kops would have approved of our dash across town. Reveling in his role as the lead driver, our chauffeur/best man Wah Kong, chose a meandering route through suburban neighborhoods and busy thoroughfares. Ba, himself no slouch at the wheel, was hot on our heels, gesticulating and bellowing in both English and Vietnamese, trying to pass us. Each time he attempted to take the lead, Wah waved cheerfully and swerved across Ba's path. "No wedding today without us," Wah laughed, "so why should we be second to anyone?"

I had no problems with Wah's sharing the joy of our evening. He was, after all, the first of Lac's students in America to achieve a black belt. Wah had assumed a premier role in our extended family of the dojo. On several occasions he had, possibly unwittingly, played Cupid for the shy master and me. There had been only one serious problem with Wah's participation in our wedding: his favorite lemon-yellow

suit and the positively inhuman pleasure he derived from wearing it. The first time my dad saw Wah in this suit, he remarked, "You know, Paula, when you were little, we had a '49 Studebaker with seat covers just that color. Good car, ran great, but those seat covers . . . " Fortunately, for this day Wah kept his promise to be more sedately attired.

As he continued to keep Ba boxed in behind us, Wah babbled in a most uncharacteristic manner, maintaining an incessant, one-sided dialogue designed to soothe rattled nerves. Calmed a bit, I faded into my own private thoughts, tuning in, then out, catching a phrase here, a punch line there.

How wide was this gulf I was crossing, during this ride, into this new life?

As a black-eyed-peas-and-cornpone child of deep southern traditionalists, I grew up in a cocoon of insular prejudice. I'm certain I felt that other races were somehow not like me. I must have accepted the notion that "white was right," that God had blessed me more than he had others, probably because I am the enviable blue-eyed blonde. I never associated with anyone who "wasn't like me." And racial poppycock was only a part of this unexamined mindset. Any foods not Southern fried or swimming in milk gravy were foreign, therefore suspect. "Integration" was a four-syllable, if not four-letter, word coined by radical Yankees who had no real understanding of dignity or decorum. And now these attitudes seemed as strange and incomprehensible to me as this new life I was entering through marriage.

While I lived in my distorted world, a profoundly different one was developing some 10,000 miles away: Lac's world, so antithetical to mine that it seems miraculous for our paths ever to cross, let alone merge.

While I was being trained and baptized into a fundamentalist Southern Baptist Church, Lac was being offered to Buddhist gods to insure the health of this strong-willed, hard-to-handle child.

While I was parading in the Cotton Carnival procession costumed as a cotton blossom, Lac was marching in the *Tet Thrung Thu* festival, dressed in *ao dai* and carrying the traditional cellophane lantern.

While I was learning to waterski in the tributaries of the Mississippi, Lac was gleefully skinny-dipping in the branches of the Mekong River.

While I was entering (and occasionally winning) track meets at the neighborhood park, Lac was entering (and always winning) international karate tournaments.

While my parents were predicting that I would be the first grandchild on either side to complete college, Lac's grandfather was predicting that he would marry a "white-haired" woman (interpreted to mean aged, not blond!) and would die on foreign soil.

While I was wearing black arm bands in anti-war rallies, Lac's helicopter was being shot down over the DMZ. He had come to the U.S. in 1972, for flight training and to perfect his English.

But most significantly, while I was living amidst attitudes of prejudice and racism, Lac was learning the balance of Yin and Yang, the blend of opposites for perfect harmony.

This man Lac was definitely not like me.

As if sharing my thoughts and reflecting on our differences, Lac squeezed my hand tightly, erasing the thoughts of my past years. "That was before," his smile said. "Our life begins today." If I had any last, lingering doubts, they flowed away like phantoms of a dream.

I began to take an interest in our parade, which, by now, had become a blur of vibrant colors, earthy aromas, an elaborate orchestration of sensations. An early morning rain, to the Vietnamese an omen of fertility, had cleansed the air. I inhaled deeply and tried to "compartmentalize," to force my nervousness into a mental "drawer" for consideration later, at some more convenient time. Obviously Lac was far more adept at this Oriental skill than I was, for his composure—whether real or feigned—was unruffled throughout the lengthy ceremony and reception.

We arrived at the house of Ma and Ba and were greeted by nearly one hundred well-wishers who lined either side of the sidewalk to applaud our entrance. Forming a wedding processional, we walked into the house. Only later did I learn that traditionally the roast pig is borne aloft, leading the way. With no pig for leadership, Wah assumed the role and pranced along the path, like a cocky drum major leading his band.

After squeezing the guests into two tiny rooms, Ba majestically lifted both hands to heaven and demanded silence. The milling about and rustling of silk *ao dai* subsided, and Ba began an imposing speech in Vietnamese welcoming his honored guests to the marriage of his son. Next he introduced one Mr. Phuc (prounounced *Fook*, please), the respected elder of the community who was to perform the ceremony. But first, he too wished to speak, at length, on the beauty of marriage, the commitment involved, the duties of both husband and wife. Mr. Phuc offered his benediction, speaking first in Vietnamese, then in halting English.

As Mr. Phuc led the way, Lac and I were ushered toward the family altar. I trembled as I began the thousand-year-old tradition, fearful that I would forget some, or all, of the myriad of instructions drilled into me during our several rehearsals. Almost mechanically, I knelt before the altar. Ah! I remembered to fold the *ao dai* under my knees as I sank down. So far, so good. Oh, how I prayed that I looked as graceful as the exquisite Vietnamese woman who had instructed me.

From the corner of my eye, I watched Lac, awaiting his cue to bow the obligatory three times before the altar. As Mr. Phuc monotoned the formal vows in his native language, my focus snapped. My mind wandered aimlessly about in an effort to impress the scene on my memory. Incense burned before a statue of Buddha, its musky flavor permeating the room. Flickering candlelight cast distorted shadows on the walls. Elaborate characters of red and gold proclaimed fortune and happiness in Chinese.

Both my dad and Ba were wearing their finest suits, and either could have been the chief executive officer of a large company. A real contrast emerged, however, between our mothers. Lac's mom, resplendent in a home-made *ao dai* of beige silk, gazed stoically into some personal distance throughout the proceedings. Her long, long hair, ebony black with not a trace of gray, was coiled in a braided knot atop her head. Mom, on the other hand, had selected her designer label aquamarine dress to complement her auburn, meticulously styled hair. Never once did her eyes leave me as I continued the ceremony that was granting

me entrance into a new culture, and one that was so alien to her own.

Before I could try, with a smile, to reassure my mom that the doors swinging open in this ceremony would not close behind me, Lac's light touch indicated that I must perform THE BOW. An intricate maneuver meant for a tiny, delicate woman, The Bow is done from a kneeling position. With hands folded in front of herself, she bends from the waist, touching her forehead to the floor. To complicate matters, I could foresee my *khan dong* tumbling off my head, rolling across the floor, and coming to rest at the legs of some strict Oriental matron. Besides dishonoring the legendary warrior princess who first wore *khan dong*, I would also be branded a graceless outsider with no dignity.

Fortunately, no such calamity occurred. I did three of the bows, performed slowly and methodically, and they were later pronounced perfect by my husband, marginal, but promising, by the remainder of the community. After completing more bows to the ancestral spirits, I was allowed to rise for the remainder of the sequence of bows—three to our parents and three to the guests. Finally Lac and I lighted incense to the spirits, bowing again as we placed the sticks into the holder. With this symbolic sacrifice, our wedding was concluded—no wedding kiss, no exchange of rings, no "I-pronounce-you's." Mr. Phuc did, however, present us to our guests: "It is my great pleasure to introduce you to Mr. and Mrs. Lac Van Tran." When the applause died down, he continued, "As representative of the bride and groom and their parents, may I invite you to share their joy by joining us in the wedding feast?"

Although the food was ready, several more traditions had to be honored prior to its being served. First, more speeches and more gifts. Each family approached Lac and me, apparently according to some loosely structured social standing that was not at all clear to me. Usually presenting us with an envelope, the man of the family would deliver a carefully prepared speech, then turn to acknowledge the applause. One guest, Uncle Aaron on Mother's side, found this such an agreeable procedure that he tried to develop a stand-up routine on the spot. In comedy, however, jokes delivered in a language that most of the audience does not understand usually lay an egg. Nonetheless, the would-be comic *did* receive a round of good-natured applause when he sat down.

The Vietnamese are a very generous people, and a person's worth is often equated with the value of gifts that are presented. In fact, a Vietnamese family will go into debt to maintain their status in the opinions of their guests. So while I was surprised at the extravagance of our many gifts, Lac simply smiled and whispered, "We'll be returning them—in full measure. It's a great cycle we've begun tonight."

At the end of the sequence of speeches, I made my way to the kitchen to help the women with the food. Only vaguely aware that the noise and festivity of the throng were waning and being replaced with a sense of expectation, I offered my aid to Ma. As she was shooing me from her domain, a small boy about three years old grabbed the back of my gown. Turning to find out what had caught my dress, I knelt and hugged this small Oriental cherub. With that a loud roar rose from the audience! They had been eagerly awaiting this event, in which I had selected the sex of my first-born child! From that moment on, the Vietnamese community were quite confident that the first child of Lac and Paula would be a son. (You can check the accuracy of their prediction in Chapter V.)

I had eaten nothing all day and was eager to begin the feast. Ma and several women of the community had been preparing this repast for two days, and the aromas were almost overpowering. To my horror, I learned that my prescribed role as bride was to serve, not to eat! Would this topsy-turvy day never end? By now I was thankful that Ba had only short notice to plan this wedding, lest I be washing down the elephants or splitting coconuts with an axe. One solace was that Lac was expected to help serve the food, also. "Good," I thought, "justice at last."

People who had not attended the wedding found their way to the banquet, for Ma's reputation as a cook is legend. Lac and I found ourselves serving over two hundred people before we were allowed to join the feasting ourselves.

Vietnamese Banquet

1. Pork, Pineapple, and Tomato Soup *(Thit Heo Xao Ca Va Thom)*
2. Pork in Cabbage Rolls Soup *(Canh Thit Goi La Cai)*
3. Shrimp Toast *(Banh Tom)*
4. Shrimp Balls *(Tom Xiu Mai)*
5. Vietnamese Meat Loaf *(Trung Chung Thit Heo)*
6. Deep-fried Drumsticks *(Dui Ga Chien)*
7. Spring Rolls *(Cha Gio)*
8. Shrimp Rolls with Fresh Vegetables *(Goi Cuon)*
9. Lemon Beef Salad *(Bo Uop Chanh)*
10. Lac's Pork *(An original recipe)*
11. Charcoal Broiled Meatballs *(Nem Nuong)*
12. Beef in Grape Leaves *(Thit Bo Cuon La Luop)*
13. Ginger Chicken *(Ga Uop Gung)*
14. Ginger Fish Sauce *(Nuoc Mam Gung)*
15. Fried Rice *(Com Chien)*

Thit Heo Xao Ca Va Thom
(Pork, Pineapple, and Tomato Soup)

½	lb. boneless pork loin
2	Tbs. fish sauce
2	Tbs. cooking oil
1½	cup pineapple, peeled, cored, chopped
2	tomatoes, cut into thin wedges
2	large shallots, thinly sliced
¼	cup minced fresh coriander leaves

Make thin slices of the pork, cutting across the grain of the meat. In a bowl, combine the pork with 4 tsp. of the fish sauce. Cover and let marinate for at least 15 minutes. In the meantime, heat the oil over high heat in a deep saucepan. Add the pork, pineapple, tomatoes, and shallots; saute the mixture for 2 minutes. Add 5 cups of water, bring to a boil, and add the salt, remaining fish sauce, and the coriander leaves. Remove from heat and serve at once.

Serves: 6.

Canh Thit Goi La Cai
(Pork in Cabbage Rolls Soup)

½	lb. ground pork	½	gal. water
1	egg, beaten	2	tsp. salt
¼	cup chopped onion	½	tsp. MSG
½	tsp. black pepper	½	tsp. vegetable oil
1	small cabbage	½	tsp. sugar
1	bunch green onions		
1	16-oz. can chicken broth		

Place ground pork, egg, onion, pepper in a mixing bowl and knead until smooth. Refrigerate while preparing the cabbage. Peel cabbage carefully to separate whole leaves. Rinse and drain. Bring a small pot of water to a boil and remove from heat. Soak the cabbage leaves and tops of green onions in the hot water long enough to soften them (approx. 3 minutes). Drain. Chop lower half of green onion bunch and set aside for garnish. When leaves are cool enough to handle, drop pork mixture onto cabbage leaf using a teaspoon. Roll into 3″ rolls and bind with the green onion tops. In a large pot, pour in the chicken broth and water; bring to boil. Drop in cabbage rolls and cook for 15 minutes. Add seasonings to taste and cook for 10-15 minutes. To serve, add black pepper and chopped green onion. May be served over cooked and drained rice noodles.

Hint: You may substitute lean ground beef and beef broth for the pork and chicken broth.

Serves: 4-6.

Banh Tom
(Shrimp Toast)

12 shrimps, cleaned and deveined
½ cup flour
1 tsp. shrimp paste
2 eggs
1 tsp. salt
¼ tsp. pepper
½ tsp. garlic powder
1 tsp. melted butter
6 slices French bread
2 tsp. fresh cilantro, crushed
3-4 Tbs. cooking oil

Cut off and discard the crusts from the bread pieces, cut them in half. Set aside for the moment. Split shrimps lengthwise. Mix salt, pepper, and garlic and add the shrimp pieces. Coat well. Let stand while you prepare the batter; beat eggs, then add the shrimp paste and melted butter. (Yes, I know it *does* seem absurd to add shrimp flavoring when you're using the real thing. But they do.) Now dip each shrimp into the flour, coating it completely. Using chopsticks or tongs, dip one side of the bread into the batter, take out, and place the floured shrimp onto the unbattered side of the bread. Spread the shrimp across the surface. Then spoon a small amount of batter onto the top of the bread. Sprinkle with cilantro. Bring oil to high heat in skillet. Place shrimp-and-bread together face-down in the hot oil and fry on each side for approximately 2 minutes, or until golden brown. Drain and serve hot. Excellent with hot mustard.

Yield: 12 pieces.

Tom Xiu Mai
(Shrimp Balls)

  ½ lb. cleaned shrimp
  ¼ lb. lean ground beef
  ¼ tsp. potato starch
  ½ tsp. MSG
  1 tsp. salt
  ½ tsp. black pepper
  1 tsp. gingerroot, crushed (or powdered gingerroot)
  ¼ tsp. garlic

Chop shrimp into small pieces and mix thoroughly with ground beef, potato starch, MSG, salt, pepper, gingerroot, and garlic. Place mixture in the blender and grind until it shows a clay-like consistency. Remove from blender and form the mixture into small, tight balls, 1 to 1½" in diameter. Steam for 35-45 minutes. Can be served with hoisin sauce or fish sauce, or on decorative toothpicks, if you like.

Yield: 25-30 meatballs.

Trung Chung Thit Heo
(Vietnamese Meat Loaf)

8-10 fresh mushrooms
½ cup bean threads
4 green onions, finely chopped
1 small onion, coarsely chopped
1½ lb. ground pork
2 Tbs. fish sauce
1 tsp. salt
1 Tbs. potato starch
pepper to taste
3 eggs

Soak bean threads in warm water for 10 minutes; chop into 2-3″ pieces. Clean and chop mushrooms; mix with bean threads, onion, green onions, and ground pork, blending well. Next add fish sauce, seasonings, and potato starch and mix all thoroughly. Beat the eggs in a small bowl, then add to pork mixture and blend well. Then place in an uncovered casserole and put in the top half of a steamer with water in the bottom. Bring to a hard boil and steam for 20-30 minutes, or until the meat is done throughout. Serve with rice.

Serves: 4-6.

Dui Ga Chien
(Deep-fried Drumsticks)

      6 chicken drumsticks
      1 cup rice flour
      2 cups water
      1 tsp. salt
      1 tsp. MSG (optional)
     ½ tsp. pepper
      2 Tbs. green onions, chopped
   2-3 cups cooking oil

Clean drumsticks and remove skin. In a large mixing bowl, blend flour, water, salt, MSG, pepper, and green onions until the batter has a smooth consistency. Drop the drumsticks in the batter, coating well. Let stand while the oil heats up in a large skillet or wok. Deep-fry the drumsticks until a golden brown, 12-15 minutes. Serve with fish sauce.

Yield: 6.

Cha Gio
(Spring Rolls)

Note: This Vietnamese specialty is totally unlike the Chinese egg roll; spring rolls are filled predominantly with meats and are wrapped in thin, crispy shells. I recommend either the Doll brand or the Thai lumpia, which can be found in Oriental food stores.

6-8 carrots, cleaned and grated
1 large onion, chopped very fine
1 lb. of bean sprouts, cleaned and broken into smaller pieces
4 garlic cloves, crushed and minced
1½ lb. lean ground round
4 black mushrooms (or 8 oz. regular mushrooms)
3 eggs, + 1 beaten egg to seal wrappers
1 Tbs. salt
2 Tbs. fish sauce
2 tsp. pepper
1 tsp. MSG (optional)

Soak black mushrooms (if these are used) for 15 minutes. Then clean and chop mushrooms into small pieces. Combine with carrots, onion, bean sprouts and garlic in a large bowl. Mix very well. Grind up the meat in a food processor, then add to the vegetables. Add seasonings to taste. Then beat in the 3 eggs; blend well. Roll and seal with the beaten egg. (See the illustration.) Deep-fry for 18-20 minutes or until the meat is cooked through. Stand upright

Spring Rolls – *(continued)*

in a colander lined with paper towels to drain. Serve hot with fish sauce and pickled vegetables (see page 121).

Note: Because I'm (still) the impatient Westerner, I hate to spend so much time over a wok frying 50 spring rolls. So I have learned a cheater's technique — I do not grind the raw meat in the food processor. Instead, I saute it lightly, in a small skillet crumbling it as it cooks, then drain carefully. This process cuts the frying time in half. I also like my foods very spicy, so I add a handful of crushed red peppers to my mixture. Everyone loves them so much that I often give "gift packs" of spring rolls for Christmas. In addition, other Vietnamese cooks I know add chicken breasts, shrimp pieces, and ground pork for different flavors.

Yield: 45-50 rolls.

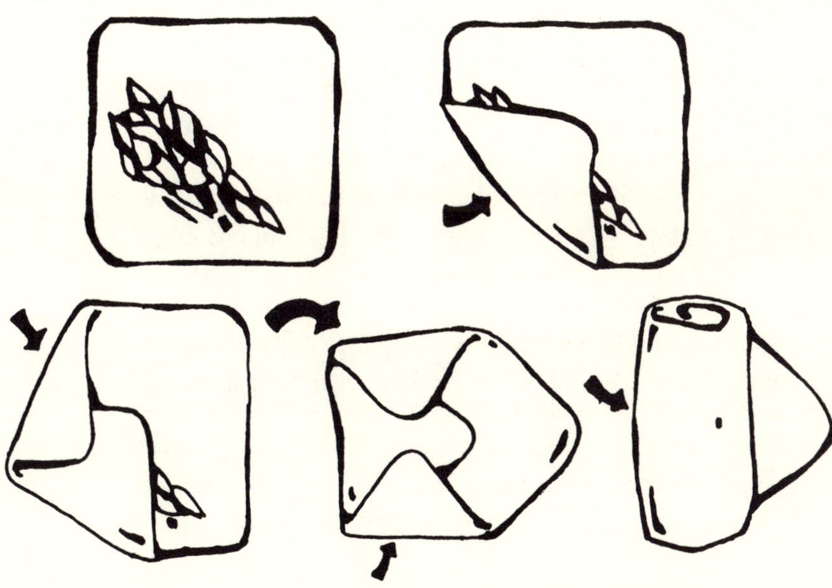

Goi Cuon
(Shrimp Rolls with Fresh Vegetables)

Note: Occasionally called "Summer Rolls".

      1 package clear edible rice paper
     ½ lb. lean pork
     ½ lb. shrimp, cleaned and deveined
      1 bundle Chinese parsley or cilantro
      1 head lettuce, cut into small pieces
      4 green onions, cut into 2-3″ pieces
      1 package of vermicelli rice noodles
    3-4 oz. mint leaves

Boil the pork until done, approximately 25 minutes. Then slice into very thin strips. Next boil the shrimp, approximately 3-5 minutes; cut into halves lengthwise. Then boil the noodles 2-3 minutes, rinse, drain. Dip the rice paper into water very quickly, no longer than a second or two. (A longer method, but one you may wish to use until you are comfortable with the rice paper, is to wet each one separately with a spray bottle of water.) Lay the rice paper on a flat surface, such s a cutting board. Then on one edge put 5-7 strands of noodles, a strip of pork, some shrimp pieces (to preference), and the lettuce, onion, cilantro, and mint. Roll it as you would an egg roll, being careful to wrap the rice paper very tightly over the fillings. Serve with fish sauce or hoisin sauce with a sprinkle of peanuts.

Yield: 24 rolls.

Bo Uop Chanh
(Lemon Beef Salad)

    1 medium cucumber, peeled and thinly sliced
    1 small onion, thinly sliced
    1 tsp. salt
    ½ lb. lean, boneless beef (sirloin, top round, etc.)
       or
    2 cups thinly sliced cold cooked beef
    2 Tbs. salad oil
    1 large lemon
    1 tsp. sugar
    1 cup shredded carrots
    1 cup thinly sliced celery
    ½ cup chopped roasted peanuts

Combine cucumber, onion, and salt; cover and refrigerate for 1 hour. Drain thoroughly and discard liquid. While mixture is in refrigerator, prepare the beef by cutting in strips and stir-frying it for approximately 2-3 minutes. Remove from heat and let cool. (Or use cold "left-over" beef.) Next, remove the thin peeling of one lemon with a vegetable peeler. Cut the peel into thin 1″ long strips. Juice the lemon. Mix together 3 Tbs. of juice, sugar, and peel. Pour over cucumber and onion mixture, add beef and mix together. Cover and refrigerate, stirring occasionally, for 1 to 4 hours. Just before serving, mix carrots, celery and peanuts with the beef mixture. Salad is ready to serve.

Serves: 4.

*Lac's Pork

1 packet Noh's Char Siu powder
(available in Oriental food stores)
½ cup sesame oil
1 Tbs. fish sauce
2 cups water
2 finely chopped green onions
2 garlic pods, crushed
1 tsp. Mei Yen or MSG (optional)
3 lbs. center-cut pork chops or lean spare ribs
½ head lettuce, separated
2 cucumbers

Prepare marinade by combining Char Siu mix with sesame oil, water and fish sauce. Next add the seasonings and mix well. Cut meat from bone and trim fat. Drop pork into the marinade, thoroughly coating each piece. Refrigerate at least two hours, preferably overnight. Then barbecue over a charcoal grill or broil in the oven until well done. Serve very thinly sliced over a bed of crisp lettuce and cucumbers. Excellent with steamed rice or on French bread.

Note: The remainder of the marinade may be heated and poured over the pork immediately before serving.

Serves: 3-4.

**Lac won first place in a cooking contest for this original recipe (1985).*

Nem Nuong
(Charcoal Broiled Meatballs)

½ lb. lean pork (or substitute bacon)
½ lb. lean round steak
1 stalk lemongrass
1 tsp. garlic, thinly sliced
¼ cup fish sauce

Using the flat side of a butcher knife or cleaver, pound the stalk of lemongrass to soften it, then slice it into thin pieces. Mix the garlic and lemongrass into the fish sauce and stir well. Slice the pork into thin, bacon-like strips. Next slice the beef into thin strips. Place the beef and pork strips in the fish sauce mixture and refrigerate for 2-3 hours. Lay the pork on a flat surface, then put a strip of beef on top of it. Roll up both strips together, lengthwise. Pierce with a skewer. Four to six may be placed on each stick. Charcoal broil these over a medium hot flame for 10-15 minutes. Baste with the fish sauce mixture as they cook.

Yield: 15.

Thit Bo Cuon La Luop
(Beef in Grape Leaves)

   1 lb. lean ground beef
3-4 garlic cloves, minced or pressed
   2 tsp. fish sauce (see p. 9)
   2 tsp. fresh ginger, minced
  ½ tsp. sugar
      a dash of pepper, to taste
  ¼ cup green onion, finely chopped
 25 (approximately) canned grape leaves

Rinse grape leaves in hot water; then drain. Mix together all of the seasonings with ground beef. Lay the leaf on a cutting board, vein side up, stem end toward you. Snip off stem. Place a generous tablespoonful of meat mixture close to the stem; pat into the shape of a log. Fold the sides of the leaf over the mixture, then roll the leaf away from you. Roll in this manner until all the mixture is used. Run a skewer through the center of several rolls. These appetizers may be prepared in advance and refrigerated until you are ready to broil or barbeque them. If charcoal is used, place about six inches from medium hot coals for 10-12 minutes; the meat should lose its pink color inside. Serve with the following dipping sauce.

Beef In Grape Leaves — *(continued)*

SAUCE

    4 Tbs. fish sauce (or substitute soy sauce)
    ½ cup of water
    2 Tbs. vinegar
    2 tsp. sugar
  ½-¾ tsp. crushed red peppers
    2 cloves of garlic, minced

In a medium mixing bowl, stir sauce ingredients together. Then stir in 2-3 Tbs. of finely shredded ginger and 2 Tbs. of finely shredded carrots. Cover and refrigerate until ready for use.

Yield: Approx. 25 rolls with ¾ cup dipping sauce.

Ga Uop Gung
(Ginger Chicken)

1   2-inch piece of fresh ginger, ground **or**
2   Tbs. powdered ginger
½   medium onion, cut into very thin slices
2   tsp. chili paste, to taste
1   tsp. salt
½   tsp. pepper
1   tsp. garlic powder
2   tsp. Maggi seasoning
½   tsp. MSG (optional)
4   chicken breasts
2   Tbs. oil

Skin and debone breasts; then cut them into bite-sized pieces. Heat the cooking oil in a skillet, then stir in the chicken strips. Saute for 3-4 minutes, then add salt, pepper, ginger, garlic powder, Maggi seasoning, and MSG. Stir until the chicken meat is golden. (You may need to add water to keep from sticking.) When the chicken is done, stir in the chili paste and onion. Cook for 2-3 more minutes, until the onions change color and become clear. Serve over a bed of rice, with Ginger Fish Sauce.

Serves: 4.

Nuoc Mam Gung
(Ginger Fish Sauce)

    4 tsp. gingerroot, peeled and minced
  2-3 large red chili peppers, minced
    2 garlic cloves, crushed
    3 tsp. sugar
    5 Tbs. fish sauce
    2 Tbs. lime juice
  ¼ cup of water

Pound the gingerroot into a paste; then add the peppers, garlic, and sugar and pound entire mixture into a paste. Pour in the fish sauce, the water and the lime juice. Mix well. Cover and refrigerate.

Yield: Approximately 1 cup.

Com Chien
(Fried Rice)

2 cups (uncooked) long-grain rice	4-5 Tbs. soy sauce
3 green onions, finely chopped	3 eggs
2 garlic cloves, crushed and minced	4-5 drops of yellow food coloring (if desired)
cooking oil	6 oz. frozen peas and carrots

any meat you may wish to add (cooked pork, chicken, seafood, all cut in very tiny pieces

To two cups of rice add 3 cups of water in large sauce pan. Bring to a boil over a high heat. Cover and turn heat to low. Steam for 20 minutes, then remove from heat. Set aside, but do not uncover until you are ready to fry the rice. In the meantime, prepare all other ingredients. In a very large skillet or a wok, heat approximately 3-4 Tbs. of cooking oil over a high heat. Reduce heat to medium. Lightly saute onions and garlic. Then pour in rice, which should be very dry. Using chopsticks or a spatula, saute rice, constantly stirring to separate. Add the eggs and stir vigorously to be certain the egg does not all settle in one area of the dish. Add soy sauce and food coloring if used. When the texture of the rice is right and all the grains are separate, then add the frozen peas and carrots. Reduce heat to low and continue cooking. Last, add whatever meats you choose and cover until ready to serve. **Serves:** 10-12.

Note: When my mother-in-law plans big dinners, she always prepares her rice the day ahead of time and refrigerates it. Thus, she is assured that it will definitely be dry enough for cooking the next day.

III
"Good Morning, Lac"

Lac and I had meticulously planned what promised to be an idyllic honeymoon in the lovers' hideaway of Acapulco. Our travel agent, a well-meaning young woman who probably watched a lot of late-night UHF television, assured us that "not even Hawaii" is as romantic as this "jewel of Mexico." Besides, she pointed out, it is infinitely more affordable. Romantic sounded nice, but cheap came out the same in both English and Vietnamese, so we borrowed $1000 and pulled together the perfect package. We agonized over decisions about which add-on's would contribute to the fulfillment of our fantasies. Rental of pink jeeps? A bit pricey, that. A side trip to Taxco? Too time consuming. The "love-boat tour"? Ah, now this looked encouraging. I could imagine the gentle roll of the ocean and the sea breezes caressing our faces as we strolled the decks hand-in-hand. How much? Thirty dollars? A mere bagatelle for the glamour I envisioned.

The last ocean cruise Lac had taken, however, was as a boat person fleeing Vietnam. This experience left him with no enthusiasm for nautical outings. "But look at the map," I cried. "That was the South China Sea; this is not far from the Gulf of California." Lac was no fool: "It's still the Pacific Ocean. Besides, it's water, lots of water, isn't it? No thanks!" The travel agent went to work on him and Lac finally gave in when he saw how much I really wanted this half-day cruise. After all, what could possibly go wrong on so short a boat ride?

So here we were, shuffling through customs in Acapulco, and confronting one of those officials whose gaze lowers the room temperature about twenty degrees. With a twisting motion of his wrist and a gesture at our bags, he ordered us to unlock our luggage. Lac, matching him stare for stare, laid the luggage on the counter and produced the keys. Then he handed the keys to me. As I fumbled with the locks, Lac ambled casually away, indulging a newly-found fascination with the Aztec paintings on the wall. His unspoken wish, it seemed, was for me to make the situation—and the customs agent, pencil-thin moustache and all—disappear. Only after thorough exposure of hair rollers, tanning oils, dental floss, and other unmentionables (including a stash of peanut butter) were we motioned to freedom. And only then did Lac rematerialize, help me to gather up our bags and hail a taxi.

Our chauffeur, Manuel, must have graduated with honors from the Kamikaze Driving Academy. Even Lac, a former military aviator, was unnerved by glimpses of terrified pedestrians and the enraged faces of other drivers. As the cab slid to a halt in front of the hotel, I thanked whatever gods watch over honeymooners and promised three sticks of incense as soon as we got settled.

I was delighted to find that our bungalow, despite being a part of a poverty package, sat half-way up the mountain, with its private pool and deck overlooking the ocean. Twice daily, the groundskeeper floated fresh blooms of crimson and white hibiscus flowers in the pool. Heavily laden vines interlaced the fences on either side of our deck, insuring privacy; their delicate fragrances hinted of tropical rain forests. Each morning I awoke to find Lac sitting on the deck in quiet meditation as the day dawned around him. The scene reminded him so much of his homeland that he spoke of Vietnam more frequently and more freely than he had ever before in our three years together.

All the pressure was forgotten, as we lay by the pool, entranced by the song of the Sirens and lethargic from the lotus blossoms we had consumed that tasted suspiciously of peanut butter on whole wheat. Not even the daily rains (which our travel agent forgot to mention) could dampen the joy of our first private time together.

It took the much-longed-for "love boat" cruise to do that.

We awoke the morning of the cruise to the sound of rain—more rain!—on the roof of our bungalow. *"Troi oi!"* Lac cheered, as he flung open the French doors to glory in the redemptive downpour. "No way we can go on that cruise today; guess they'll cancel it!" Then recognizing my dejection, he amended, "Isn't that a shame?"

I phoned the number listed on the tickets to ask about refunds or a rescheduled cruise. "Oh, no-o-o-o, Senora," the lady trilled. "Theese ees Au-gust in Aca-pull-co. Ees rain ev'ry day. Treep, she go, si! Boat cover, si!" Of course, a covered boat. It would take more than a furious downpour to keep us from the charms of Neptune!

We arrived a few minutes before the scheduled departure. However, the only craft at the dock was a large, unkempt, rusty scow. So why was there a line of people waiting to board?

"Oh, no! Oh, dear! That surely cannot be our boat. We're going on a *cruise*! Ours must be at another pier, Lac."

"Nope, Paula. This proud beauty is your Love Boat."

I ran up to the nearest woman in line and asked,

"Hable ingles, Senora?"

She spoke enough to confirm that this boat was the harbor cruise. What was more, we had better hurry to get in line to board.

"C'mon, Paula. We're here; let's take that cruise." Lac took my hand and maneuvered us through the crowd to await our turn to board. There's no use judging a boat by its cover.

On the second level we found a bar and a dance floor. Lac asked if I wanted a drink, but since the line to the bar already extended across the deck, I declined. No waiters aboard this ship of fools. We chose two seats against the railing, which offered a perfect view of the shore as we sailed along, and also the dance floor. Lac, who will not dance, turned his attention to the gyrating couples and was stunned to observe several women dancing together, and closely. In Vietnamese culture, both men and women will freely hold hands with members of their own gender; there are no sexual connotations involved. But the open intimacy of these women bewildered Lac.

He was engrossed by this scene and blind to activities around him, a rare lapse for this observant martial artist. He had not seen a crew member costumed as a pirate who was sneaking up on passengers, then placed a chrome-plated machete to their throats while an accomplice took a Polaroid snapshot. I had been watching this money-making ruse, but filed it away as just one more aberration of this glorious trip.

A few minutes later the "pirate" grabbed Lac from behind, catching him totally off-guard. His defenses snapping alert, Lac seized the man's wrist in an Aikido hold and disarmed him. The machete was sent clattering away across the deck where the dancers leaped about to avoid it. Lac had his assailant in a painful lockhold and, still unaware that the whole thing was a gimmick, was about to send the poor man over the rail.

"Don't, Lac!" I screamed. "Don't hurt him! It's all an act!" Lac paused to consider this development, but clearly was unconvinced that threatening people with machetes was a possible source of amusement. The pirate, who had met resistance for the first time in

his career as a corsair, knew that only a thread suspended him from a swimming lesson.

Lac now saw the man with the camera, who was standing, mouth agape, and stunned at the impossibly quick reactions of this tourist, terrified that his partner was on the verge of being sent flying into the sea. "Another of Paula's wonderful surprises," Lac must have thought. Just then the camera clicked and whirred as the exposed print popped out.

Lac took a second to return, mentally, to the cruise and carefully unhanded the pirate and smoothed down the man's shirt. Lac walked through the stunned crowd of frozen dancers to pick up the machete. He walked back to the pirate and handed it to the man, just as the throng, interpreting the near-disaster as a bit of planned entertainment laid on for their amusement, burst into appreciative applause.

We had earmarked no special funds for unauthorized photographs, but the photographer timidly approached Lac and held out the picture at arm's length. The photograph showed Lac's hands only as a blur and the pirate's face stunned and contorted in astonishment.

That did it for me in paradise. We learned our lesson well: Paradise is in the eye of the beholder. We were not grieved to head for San Antonio. Especially when we arrived and found Ba waiting for us at the airport. He drove us not home to our apartment, but to his house, for Ma had been concerned that we had eaten virtually nothing at her reception dinner. She welcomed us with some of Lac's favorite dishes—which have since become mine as well.

Some Favorite Dishes

1. Cucumber Soup *(Canh Dua Leo)*
2. Barbequed Drumsticks *(Dui Ga Nuong)*
3. Sauteed Chicken Livers, Hearts, and Gizzards *(Long Ga Xao Gung)*
4. Boiled Crab *(Cua Luot)*
5. Vietnamese Chicken Salad *(Goi Ga)*
6. Stir-fried Shrimp/Crab *(Tom Rang Muoi/Cua Rang Muoi)*
7. Shrimp Omei *(An original recipe)*
8. Beef and French-fried Potatoes *(Thit Bo Xao Khoai Tay)*
9. Tomatoes Stuffed with Crab *(Ca Don Chua)*
10. Steamed Fish *(Ca Hap)*
11. Fish Lemongrass *(Ca Uop Xa)*
12. Sauteed Pork and Shrimp *(Mang Xao Thit Heo)*
13. Octopus with Vegetables *(Muc Xao)*
14. Bittermelon *(O Qua)*

Canh Dua Leo
(Cucumber Soup)

NOTE: This tasty soup is very inexpensive to prepare and requires only 30 minutes. A wonderful dinner for a working couple.

2 medium cucumbers, lightly peeled
4 chicken thighs, or breasts, cleaned and skinned
2 tsp. salt
1 tsp. pepper
1 tsp. MSG (optional)
2 tsp. sesame oil
1 Tbs. cilantro, chopped
½ small onion, chopped very finely

Chop chicken pieces into 1-3″ strips, then put into a large soup pan with ½ gallon water. Bring to a boil and allow chicken to cook until done, approximately 20-25 minutes. (As chicken cooks, skim off the foam that rises to keep the broth clear. You may need to add water as the soup cooks down.) When the soup is totally clear, stir in salt, pepper, MSG, if desired, to taste. While the soup simmers, prepare the cucumbers by slicing them lengthwise first, then cut across in ¼″ strips. After the chicken is completely cooked, add the cucumbers and quickly bring to a boil again. (Cucumbers should cook for only a minute at most.) Remove from heat, ladle into soup bowls, add ½ tsp. sesame oil, and garnish with chopped onion and cilantro to serve.

Serves: 4.

Dui Ga Nuong
(Barbequed Drumsticks)

- 6 chicken drumsticks, cleaned and skinned
- 1 tsp. lemongrass, crushed
- ¼ cup fish sauce
- ¼ tsp. MSG (optional)
- 1 clove garlic, crushed
- 1 tsp. Chinese parsley, chopped

In a mixing bowl thoroughly blend the lemongrass, fish sauce, MSG, garlic, and parsley. Drop in the drumsticks, and coat well. Cover the bowl and refrigerate for 2 hours. Cook the drumsticks on a charcoal grill over medium heat for 10-15 minutes. Each time you turn the pieces, baste with the remaining marinade.

Yield: 6.

Long Ga Xao Gung
(Sauteed Chicken Livers, Hearts, and Gizzards)

2 Tbs. cooking oil

2 onions, cut into small wedges

1 lb. chicken livers, trimmed and thinly sliced

1 lb. chicken hearts, sliced thinly

1 lb. chicken gizzards, trimmed and thinly sliced

2 Tbs. gingerroot, peeled and minced

2 Tbs. fish sauce

2 tsp. dark brown sugar

In a large skillet heat the oil over medium high flame until very hot. Saute the onion, livers, hearts, and gizzards, stirring for 2 minutes. Stir in the gingerroot, fish sauce, sugar, and 2 Tbs. of water and cook the mixture over medium low heat, stirring frequently, for 3 to 5 minutes or until the sauce is reduced slightly. Serve on a large platter, garnished with celery and carrot curls.

Serves: 6.

Cua Luot
(Boiled Crab)

2 large crabs, cleaned
1 pkg. shrimp and crab boil
1 lemon, cut into wedges
1 large onion, cut into fourths
1 3″ piece of gingerroot, thinly sliced

In a large pot, bring 2 gallons of water to a hard boil. Add the crab boil, lemon, onion, and gingerroot. Allow to boil for 15-20 minutes before adding the crabs. Then drop in the crabs and return to a full boil for 10-15 minutes. Drain and serve with fish sauce. (You may wish to drop in two white potatoes when you add the crab boil. Add a green salad, and dinner is served in 30 minutes!)

Serves: 2.

Goi Ga
(Vietnamese Chicken Salad)

        1 large frying chicken
        1 head of cabbage, finely chopped
        1 Tbs. + 1 tsp. salt
        1 medium onion, chopped very fine
        2 serrano peppers, finely chopped
        ¼ cup vinegar
        2 tsp. sugar
        2 tsp. chopped cilantro
        2 tsp. oil

Steam chicken and shred meat off bone. (Dispose of fat and skin.) Sprinkle one Tbs. of salt over cabbage and set aside. In a small skillet, heat oil to high. Stir in onion until browned. (Onions should be very crisp, not burned.) Mix vinegar, sugar, and remaining salt in a small bowl. Wash cabbage and drain on paper towels or in colander. Pour vinegar mixture over cabbage; then add peppers and cilantro. Stir in chicken pieces. This salad, like many Vietnamese salads, may be served cold or hot. Excellent over rice or noodles.

Serves: 6-8.

Tom Rang Muoi
Sauteed (Stir-fried) Shrimp

½ lb. fresh shrimp, cleaned
1 tsp. vegetable oil
1 clove garlic, thinly sliced
1 tsp. salt
1 tsp. sugar
⅛ cup water
3-4 green onions, chopped

Heat oil in small skillet over medium-high temperature; add garlic and saute lightly. Mix salt, sugar, and water. *Very carefully* add to the hot oil. Then put in the shrimp and cook until the liquid vaporizes and the mixture dries out (approximately 8 minutes). Sprinkle the onions over the shrimp. May be served individually on decorative tooth picks or on a bed of steamed rice.

Serves: 2-4.

Cua Rang Muoi
Sauteed (Stir-fried) Crab

This recipe is prepared exactly as the sauteed shrimp, except that ½ lb. of crab is substituted for the shrimp. Both dishes serve well as an appetizer or as a main dish.

Serves: 2-4.

*Shrimp Omei

Batter:
      3 lbs. large shrimp
      2 cups sifted flour
      1 egg, slightly beaten
 1½ cups water
      1 tsp. salt
      1 tsp. MSG (optional)
 1-2 tsp. green onions, chopped
        vegetable oil

Sauce:
      1 6-ounce can Mijako black soybeans *or* 1 6-ounce
        can Szechuen bean sauce
 1½ cups water
      ¼ cup soy sauce
      1 garlic clove, crushed
        small piece of gingerroot, thinly sliced
      2 green onions, chopped
      2 Tbs. vinegar
 2-3 sliced red peppers, to taste

Clean and devein the shrimp and set aside. Prepare batter by mixing all ingredients and stirring to a smooth consistency. One by one, drop the shrimp into the batter to coat thoroughly.

Shrimp Omei — *(continued)*

In the meantime mix all the ingredients for the spicy sauce and simmer in a small saucepan over a low heat, approximately 15 minutes. While the sauce simmers, quick-fry the shrimp in hot cooking oil. Drain carefully and pour the hot sauce over the shrimp. Serve immediately, over steamed rice, if desired.

NOTE: The Mijako is spicier than the Szechuen, so you may wish to omit the peppers if using the former.

This sauce is wonderful with steaks or pork. In place of the shrimp in batter, try frying par-boiled pork cubes, mushrooms, onion rings, potato slices, green peppers, okra, or other vegetables tempura-style. This zesty sauce enhances all of these.

Serves: 6.

**Lac won first place in a cooking contest for this original recipe (1983).*

Thit Bo Xao Khoai Tay
(Beef and French-fried Potatoes)

    3   large potatoes, peeled, cut in tiny strips
    1   lb. very lean round steak, sliced paper thin
    1   large onion, cut into thin wedges
    2   green onions, finely chopped
    1   large tomato, cut into small cubes
    ½   tsp. cornstarch
    ½   cup of water
  3-4   garlic cloves, crushed and minced
    3   tsp. fish sauce
    ½   tsp. pepper, or to taste
        Cooking oil

Cover bottom of a skillet with approximately ½″ of cooking oil and bring to a medium high heat. Drop in potato strips and fry until golden brown; remove, drain, and set aside. Pour off all of oil except 3-4 tablespoons. Stir the cornstarch into the water and add the fish sauce. Reheat the remaining oil in skillet and briefly sautee the onion wedges and garlic. Next add the beef and stir-fry for approximately two minutes. Then add the tomato cubes and the green onions. As you stir, add the cornstarch mixture. Cook for 3-4 more minutes, until the liquid is reduced slightly. Return potatoes to the skillet. Stir well and allow time just to heat through. Add pepper to taste. Serve.

Serves: 6-8.

Note: As a "meat and potato" person, I can highly recommend this recipe!

Ca Don Chua
(Tomatoes Stuffed with Crab)

2 large crabs, cleaned
4 firm tomatoes, slightly green
2 tsp. fish sauce
½ tsp. MSG
1 Tbs. gingerroot, sliced
1 tsp. fresh cilantro leaves, chopped
½ tsp. salt
1 tsp. potato starch
2 Tbs. cooking oil

Cut the tops off the tomatoes and core them. Rinse them out with clear water and set aside. Take all of the meat out of the crab claws and bodies and chop up finely. Add the fish sauce, MSG, gingerroot, cilantro, salt, and potato starch. Mix thoroughly. Stuff the mixture into the hollowed-out tomatoes. Coat the bottom of a baking pan with the oil to prevent sticking and bake for 20-25 minutes at 350°. Serve immediately and top with oyster sauce.

Yield: 4.

Ca Hap
(Steamed Fish)

2 large fish, cleaned
1 lime (or lemon), half of which is thinly sliced
1 tsp. salt
1 cup fish sauce
1 tsp. gingerroot, crushed
1 tsp. sugar
1 tsp. vegetable oil
1 Tbs. sliced garlic
1 Tbs. cilantro, chopped
3 cups water

Mix fish sauce, sugar, gingerroot, sliced half of lime, and cilantro in a large bowl; stir well. Marinate the fish in this mixture, cover and refrigerate for 30 minutes to an hour. Remove the fish from the bowl and pour the marinade in the bottom of a steamer. Add the water and bring to simmer. Coat the bottom of an oven-tempered casserole with oil and then put the fish in it. Set the uncovered casserole in the steamer and steam for 15-20 minutes. To serve: Put salt in a small dipping bowl and squeeze half a lime over it. Dip pieces of fish into this mixture.

Serves: 2-4.

Ca Uop Xa
(Fish Lemongrass)

      2 large redfish
      1 stalk lemongrass
      1 hot pepper, bias-sliced thinly
    ½ tsp. curry powder
      1 tsp. salt
      1 garlic clove, crushed
    2-3 Tbs. oil

Crush the stalk of lemongrass with the flat side of a cleaver, then cut it into small pieces. Clean the fish and with a sharp knife slash diagonally across the body of the fish. Mix lemongrass, curry powder, salt, and peppers. Put the redfish in the mixture, coat well, cover and refrigerate for one hour. Heat oil in a large skillet, and lightly saute the garlic. Then place the redfish in the skillet, let brown very well before turning it over. (If the fish is not very brown, it wil fall apart.) Brown well on the other side, and serve.

Serves: 2-4.

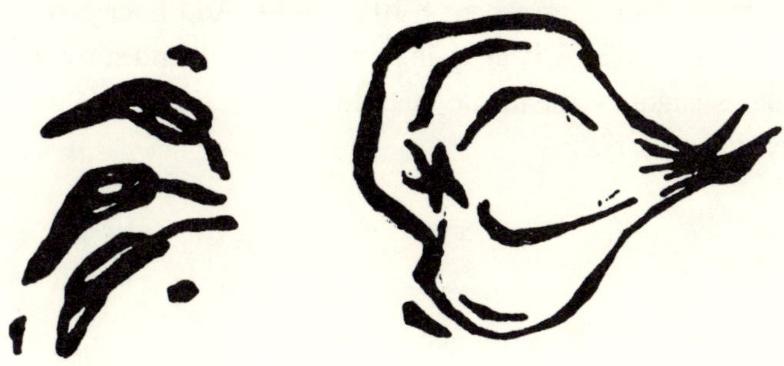

Mang Xao Thit Heo
(Sauteed Pork and Shrimp)

        3 Tbs. cooking oil
        2 small onions, thinly sliced
      3-4 hot chili peppers
        1 lb. boneless pork loin, thinly sliced
        ½ lb. pork liver, slivered (optional)
        1 lb. shelled shrimp
        1 cup bamboo shoots, drained, chopped
        2 tsp. flour dissolved in 4 Tbs. water
        4 cored tomatoes, thinly sliced
        2 Tbs. fish sauce
        5 Tbs. minced cilantro leaves

Split shrimp lengthwise, salt and pepper lightly. In a skillet heat the oil over a moderate flame until it is very hot. Add the onion, cook, and stir for 5 minutes or until golden brown. Next add the peppers, the pork loin, the pork liver (if used), the shrimp, and the bamboo shoots; cook the mixture over a moderately low heat, stirring for 8-10 minutes. Add flour mixture, tomatoes, and fish sauce, raising heat again to medium high and stirring until the sauce thickens slightly. Stir in the cilantro, then serve in a large dish. Excellent over steamed rice.

Serves: 4-6.

Muc Xao
(Octopus with Vegetables)

1 large octopus
1 cucumber
1 small onion cut into thin slices
1 small bunch of Chinese parsley
2 Tbs. cooking oil
1 garlic clove, crushed
¼ tsp. sesame oil

Clean octopus by removing the head. With sharp knife, split body and remove the insides. Peel off the outside skin. Slice the octopus into pieces approximately 1-2″. Next cut the cucumber in half lengthwise, then across in 1″ pieces. Heat cooking oil in a large skillet over medium high flame, then put in the octopus pieces. Stir-fry for 8-10 minutes. Add the vegetables, garlic and parsley, and continue cooking for 5 more minutes. Just before removing the skillet from the heat, stir in the sesame oil.

Serves: 4.

NOTE: If you want to spare yourself the joy of removing octopi heads, you can buy them already cleaned at some supermarkets.

O Qua
(Stuffed Bittermelon)

Note: The Vietnamese attribute magical powers to this very bitter tasting vegetable which fits in the palm of the hand. It is fed to pregnant women to insure the health of their babies. Although I enjoy the flavor of o qua, many of my non-Asian friends find it too sharp for their palates. In fact, if I were ever called upon to describe the taste of the color green, I would simply point to bittermelon!

6	bittermelons	¼	onion
1	lb. lean pork	2	Tbs. fish sauce
1-3	black mushrooms	1	tsp. MSG
½	packet bean threads	2	tsp. salt
	(approx. 4 oz.)	1	tsp. sugar

Soak the mushrooms in water for 10-15 minutes, until they are soft and pliable. Drain. During this period, place bean threads in a pot of boiling water for 2-3 minutes, until they become translucent. Then in a large mixing bowl, stir together the pork, mushrooms, bean threads, onions, 1 Tbs. of fish sauce and MSG. Place this mixture in a blender and mix to a clay-like consistency. Next, cut open the bittermelons, lengthwise, but cut only on one side. Clean out the seeds and wash out the cavities. Spoon mixture into the bittermelons and place them in a large saucepan. Cover with water and bring to a hard boil over medium high heat. Reduce heat to medium low. Add sugar, salt, and remaining fish sauce to water. Boil for approximately 15 minutes, or until the meat is cooked thoroughly.

Yields: 6.

IV
Chicken-Fry to Chi Hai

My wedding, with all its chaos and confusion, served as an appropriate introduction to my new culture. The honeymoon offered insights into the depths of Lac's personality. But it was our return home that provided the real education in Vietnamese life: recognition of the family as the cornerstone of the culture.

My first lesson, perhaps not too surprisingly, introduced me to the degree of male dominance that the Vietnamese find not only familiar but even comforting. It took Ma little time to surmise that my cooking strengths were confined to chicken fried steak, pan fries, and a lettuce wedge with Thousand Island dressing. So we were frequently invited to what became leisurely Sunday dinners, Vietnamese style, at Ma's. After one such meal, Lac excused himself to participate in the latest chapter of his destiny: coaching the Dallas Cowboys. Lac lay prone before the set, frequently conferring with Tom Landry and only occasionally overruling him. My patience with football in general wore thin that afternoon as two quarters dragged by on leaden cleats. I had lessons to prepare and papers to grade at home. In addition, I couldn't share in the conversation, since at my in-laws' home Vietnamese is spoken almost exclusively. Finally, I prodded Lac, "Honey, let's go home, I've got tons of work to do for classes next week."

There was no response, which is the Vietnamese way of refusing a request without ever acknowledging it.

The next time I placed myself between him and the screen, "Lac, dear, I'm ready to go home. I need to work!"

Forced to recognize my intrusion, he replied, "No, I'd like to finish this game."

"But you can finish the game at home. I *need* to work. Besides, a 15-minute quarter invariably lasts 45 minutes. You'll likely miss only three plays if we leave now."

With a martyred expression, Lac bolted upright, jerked on his shoes, then snapped, "Let's go. Now!" Bowing to the elders, I excused myself and scurried after his retreating figure to the car.

For several minutes we drove in silence, Lac's mouth all sucked up inside his face. "Lac, calm down. You're not going to miss much of the game," I attempted to placate him. "There's no need to be angry or upset."

"It's not the game," he retorted. "You argued with me in front of my parents."

Oh, Lord, another faux pas. Of course, a man loses face if his wife controls him. Why don't Asian husbands come with instruction manuals? For all of Lac's experiences in the West, and his normally untroubled view of matters, this incident affected the core of his being, his family. Never mind that *I* am part of his family now . . .

However, it is good that I learned that lesson early in our marriage. It has helped me refrain from blurting out opinions—and Western ones, at that—in areas where men supposedly reign supreme. A prime example is taxes. From the first year of our marriage I inherited the responsibility of all bookkeeping, including the computation of income taxes. In short order Ma and Ba's tax accounts also became my responsibility. To this day, every time I deliver the completed forms for their approval and signatures, Ba very studiously scans over my figures, then hands the forms to Lac for confirmation . . . Lac, this same man who would rather pet a rattlesnake than consult the instruction booklet for Form 1040A, this same man who once seriously suggested deducting our cat's vet fees as medical expenses. This man Lac—who believes a debit is a small, fluffy animal with big eyes— this man sees nothing odd about assuring Ba that *my* figures seem to be in order. And he does so, annually. As I stand by, a practiced smile across my face, Lac gazes at the form, nods his head wisely, and asserts, "Yes, Ba, it's fine." Only then will Ba affix his signature and mail the forms. And I, the Chi Hai, "the first sister," have maintained my place and given great "face" to the men of the clan. That I do the work is immaterial; that I let the men judge it is everything.

In truth, I wasn't sure that I would ever become the Chi Hai. Even though marriage to Anh Hai, first brother, theoretically guaranteed my title, my independence prior to marriage did not. We broke with the ancient tradition of a woman's leaving her home, becoming a member of her husband's family, and assuming a status determined by birth order. They already had five children at home; so were Lac, my own daughter Sunni, and I (not to mention a menagerie of pets) to move in, we would all have gone mad in a fortnight.

At first, Lac warned me that I would not want to be the Chi Hai: her role in the culture is a dubious one. Cooking, cleaning, obeying commands, the "first daughter" frequently becomes a form of personal maid for her mother-in-law. Despite this warning, I could never imagine my gentle, good-natured Ma's dominating anyone. She nurtures, never nags.

As my young brothers-and-sisters-in-law became

more comfortable in my presence, less shy in speaking with me, they gradually began calling me "Chi Hai," a giant step up from calling me nothing at all. I liked it even though I didn't fully understand why the first sister is actually called the second sister ("Hai" means two). Lac explained that in Vietnam no one in birth order is ever called "the first." The numeral one is traditionally reserved for the king.

Regardless of the motivation, "earning" my name pleased me. I had entered the family much too late to be granted a pet name which is frequently assigned to youngsters and follows them into adulthood. For instance, the youngest child in Lac's family has been called *Be*, ("Baby") from birth. Still another of her pet names is *Ut*, "the youngest member of the family." Thus my sons call fourteen-year-old Hong *Co Ut*, "the aunt who is the youngest member of the family." Other nicknames include *Ti*, or "tiny one," and *Teo*, which means "little." These are family names for two of Lac's brothers, An and Nhan, both of whom are now young adults.

As a sign of respect, other friends and acquaintances outside the immediate family circle are addressed in familial terms. For example, all of Ma's friends have now become "aunts," while Ba's cronies are "uncle" or "brother," depending upon their ages. To these elders, I have never been "Paula," always the Chi Hai, or more formally, Mrs. Lac. (A striking paradox of women's role in this culture is that they are allowed to maintain their maiden names; only those who are more Americanized now assume their husbands' surnames.)

I found that the Vietnamese never say no to anyone, about anything. They may say "yes" but mean "no" and never consider that they have been deceitful. On the contrary, they feel that a polite response is obligatory. Throughout the early days I had assumed that this trait was merely an endearing aberration peculiar to my husband, one that my careful guidance would eventually resolve. No so. As semi-official spokeswoman for the clan, I have been called upon to refuse pushy magazine salespersons, return defective merchandise, argue with arrogant auto mechanics, as well as refuse invitations — all because I have this crass, but occasionally useful, barbaric ability to say "no." They rely on me as a form of *Anh Hung*, or "big gun" when situations become crucial, yet I sometimes feel as if they have the same attitude toward me that they might have towards a battleship steaming along the coast—good to have on your side, but scary, and, because of its firepower, a trifle suspect.

My reputation for effective, even devastating salvos has in no way spared me the lesson of *nha toi cung hnu nha anh*, a Vietnamese form of "My house is your house." Six months after settling into our small two-bedroom apartment, fifteen of Lac's friends descended—unannounced—to spend the weekend in San Antonio. To be precise, there were six friends, four children, and five friends of friends, all expecting food and lodging. I hinted that there was no room to make our guests comfortable, but the leader of this boarding party brushed away my objections, declaring that there was "plenty room on floor." That night, bodies lay scattered throughout the apartment, ours included, since "nha toi cung" demands that we give up our beds to guests.

Now I am more comfortable with the Vietnamese form of hospitality. Having ten to fifteen drop in unexpectedly for a bowl of soup no longer fazes me—especially since I know that they would welcome me and a horde of my friends.

One characteristic of Vietnamese life does continue to perturb me though: timing. The Vietnamese are notoriously and constantly late. Lac claims that being late is a measure of their importance, reflecting a deep-seated concern for status. (This problem, I admit, is carefully contained within the social context. As workers and students the Vietnamese are typically prompt, energetic, and industrious. Apparently they operate, like Einsteinian relativity, under two very different concepts of time.)

Our first dinner party was planned to honor Lac's parents and the Nguyens, a couple who had supported our decision to marry when others, including a very influential Vietnamese priest, were vocal in their opinions that Lac and I were mismatched. "Good kids," the nay-sayers opined, "but foolish and impulsive." In contrast Mr. Nguyen Van Canh had spoken eloquently to our parents that crossing cultures could work, especially if we had support and understanding.

Certain that an attempt to cook Vietnamese food would convince Ma to begin annulment proceedings, I opted for my stand-by of spaghetti and meatballs. All day I cooked and cleaned, preparing for our 6:00 dinner party. By 6:30 Lac's parents had arrived, and the pasta sat in a colander, firm, fresh, ready for service.

At 7:30 the pasta remained in the colander, matted, congealed, unfit for service even as a mop. Finally, at 8:15, the Nguyens arrived, right on Vietnam time.

That incident along taught me an important lesson about Vietnam time; nevertheless, I continue to be surprised at its effects. As sponsor of the Vietnamese Student Association at the university where I teach, I was invited to a Christmas party at a small oriental restaurant. Arriving ten minutes late at 7:10, Lac and I found the building locked up. I reread the invitation; yes, right place, right evening, 7:00 p.m. We waited for 45 minutes, wrote a note to tuck into the door, then left. An hour later the president of the association telephoned, "Why didn't you come to the party?"

"But we *were* there. No one else was!"

In all earnestness, "Surely you know that 7:00 isn't *really* 7:00, don't you?"

Well, what *could* I have been thinking of?

Yet another tendency characteristic of Vietnamese people seems paradoxical from a culture otherwise so concerned with appropriate actions and graceful manners. Elders, by virtue of their age or rank, feel free to pose any question to those younger, no matter how blunt, embarrassing, or personal. For example, as Co Kim wandered through our new home, she asked, "How much did you pay for it?" Still another well-meaning "aunt" patted my stomach and inquired, "When you get baby?" By now, questions such as "how much money you make?" may well be answered, "Oh, after taxes, $250,000."

As the Chi Hai I occasionally find myself in a position of explaining, in a sense, defending, my culture. Two instances leap to mind, in the areas of medicine and of child rearing, both of which clash sharply with Western notions.

My introduction to Oriental medicine occurred when Ba severely strained his back at work. Ma, who has never learned to drive, summoned us to the house, once Ba's condition had deteriorated over several days to the point that he could not even put on his shoes. When we arrived, I noticed—then ignored — a mound of colorful cloth remnants piled on the kitchen floor. As Lac asked about Ba, the pile responded and uncovered the man crouched over a pot of steaming herbs. The odor of lemongrass and orange peel flooded the room. Ba attempted to stand, but collapsed, sprawling across the patchwork material that had covered him. I watched Lac gingerly lift his father, and to my horror noticed that his back and arms were covered with ugly glaring bruises, the likes of which I had never seen. "Good lord, Lac!" I exclaimed. "Look at Ba's back; he's been beaten!"

"No, not at all," Lac replied. "That's just medication, tiger balm. We rub it in with a coin, usually a quarter. The friction always leaves these marks on the body." Later I learned that several refugee families have been investigated for child abuse when their children appeared similarly bruised at schools.

This time the tiger balm and the herbal concoction failed to offer relief. I suggested an osteopath but Ba nixed that proposal, deciding instead on a Chinese-Vietnamese acupuncturist. Visions of needles danced in my head, yet no amount of common-sense reasoning could sway his determination. I placed the call, explained the dilemma, and agreed that we could be there in twenty minutes. After helping Ba with his shirt and shoes, Lac half-carried Ba to the car. Off we went, with me more apprehensive than Ba.

Dr. Chang greeted us personally, then assisted Ba into an examining room, after leaving me with his press clippings and a copy of a book he had published in Chinese. An hour passed, then another. Finally Ba walked out, unattended. "See," he said. "Good, no more pain." The doctor explained that Ba had suffered a pinched nerve and would need two follow-up treatments for full recovery. Giving him an envelope of herbs, he scheduled an appointment for the following week and urged him to come earlier if the pain recurred.

Despite his remarkable improvement, I determined that he should see a specialist for a complete workup. I knew that Ba had received virtually no medical care since he had arrived in the United States some 15 years earlier. At my insistence, and with Lac's support, he agreed to see an internist. Two days later we sat in the doctor's office—a *real* doctor, I believed. Taking one look at the bruised back, the doctor exclaimed, "Where did you get those contusions?"

"Not to worry," I answered for him. "It's just Oriental medicine in action. In fact, two days ago, he couldn't stand unassisted, but after only one visit to the acupuncturist, he chugged out of the office on his own steam. I was amazed!"

"You mean to tell me all *that's* going on here in San Antonio?" And he shook his head as if I had suggested that he participate in a voodoo ritual.

A second East-West clash I feel obliged to defend involves our opposing philosophies of child-rearing. As military brats, my siblings and I were taught "sir-yes-sir" obedience from our infancy. I vaguely recall "double-to-the-rear" drills in diapers and rousing to Reveille each morning. Certainly, my parents were stern, though not abusive. However, their word was never open to challenge either. In their world, children had a place, but that place was designated by parents. As a result, my theories of child-rearing naturally leaned toward authoritarian control.

This approach would not sell in Saigon. In all my years in the culture, I have never seen a child under ten being disciplined—not even so much as a scolding. On the contrary, *I* was once gently chided for attempting to prevent my five-year-old son from dismantling the toilet at his grandfather's house. "La, la,

Chi Hai," Ba intervened, "let the baby be. He's not hurting anything. He just wants to see how it works."

The paradox is that at some point in their development, these unrestrained little demons metamorphose into obedient, polite youngsters, the type even my dad would approve of. One day, tiny terrorists; the next, adolescent exemplars. How the transition occurs remains one of the seven great mysteries, but I constantly burn incense in hopes that the conversion will occur in my sons' lives as well. Soon!

Yes, cultural conversion can prove slow, often frustrating for everyone involved. After ten-plus years, I find I am still adjusting, still accommodating to a difficult but intriguing mindset. I am challenged to think, to communicate—and to cook—as a Vietnamese. Fortunately for me I have the most patient of teachers, the most accomplished of cooks as my culinary mentor. On family occasions Lac and I always arrive early, ostensibly for the Chi Hai to help prepare for our guests. At first Ma kindly assigned me innocuous tasks that are Paula-proof. These included setting the table, putting ice in the glasses, ladling foods into serving bowls—hardly responsibilities that require an accomplished cook. Later, as Ma became more comfortable with me, she began my conversion to "Oriental wife" by teaching me to cook. Ma and I have collaborated to create these menus for inexperienced cooks—or for more sophisticated chefs with limited time. Don't let their simplicity fool you; they are tasty, attractive, nutritious, and, oh yes, Paula-proof!

Soups as Everyday Meals

1. Chicken with Rice Soup *(Chao Ga)*
2. Thick Noodle Pork Soup *(Banh Canh)*
3. Sauteed Beef Soup *(Bo Kho)*
4. Meatball Soup *(Pho Bo Vo Vien)*
5. Crab Noodle Soup *(Bun Reu)*
6. Beef with Noodle Soup *(Pho Bo)*
7. Hot and Spicy Soup *(Bun Bo Hue)*
8. Barbeque and Shrimp Soup *(Hu Tieu)*
9. Sweet and Sour Fish Soup *(Canh Chua Voi Ca)*
10. Turkey Sausage and Pork Ball Noodle Soup *(Bun Moc)*
11. Pick-a-Pork Soup *(Chao Long Heo)*
12. Liver and Rice Soup *(Chao Long Ga)*
13. Duck Soup *(Vit Tiem)*
14. Boiled Duck with Ginger Rice Soup *(Chao Vit)*
15. Chicken Soup *(Bun Thang)*

A WORD ABOUT SOUPS . . .

The Vietnamese soups, unlike most soups of the Western cultures, can serve as a full meal. Generally composed of rice noodles, slivers of meats and meatballs, and vegetable garnishes, the many varieties of soups are nutritious, hearty, and delicious.

Soups are so popular among the Vietnamese people that they could well be called the unofficial national food. Indeed, just as ice cream, snow cone, and hot dog vendors roam American streets, so too in Vietnamese cities the *ong ban pho xe*, or soup man, arises at dawn, prepares huge vats of soup, and begins his daily rounds. Pushing a little cart, he meanders the village streets, his arrival announced by his rhythmic beatings on two bamboo sticks. Thus the villagers awaken to a bowl of steaming soup.

Helpful Hints for Preparing These Soups

- Always clean and wash the soup bones carefully before cooking. The Vietnamese are fanatics about "clean bones". In fact, if Lac suspects that I have been derelict in my duties, he will label my soups as "gritty"!

- Never throw away bones when you cut uncooked meats from them. Freeze them and use them for soup later.

- As the soup cooks, always skim off the foam that accumulates on the top. The clearer the soup, the better.

- During the cooking process, taste your soup broth periodically to adjust the seasonings according to your preferences.

- Almost all the Vietnamese soups are enhanced before serving by the addition of bean sprouts, thinly sliced hot peppers, green onions, juice from fresh limes or lemons, cilantro, mint, and hoisin sauce.

- Don't try to save time in preparing these soups. Often what you gain in time, you sacrifice in flavor.

Chao Ga
(Chicken with Rice Soup)

    ½ cup uncooked rice
    1 chicken, skinned, cleaned, and cut into pieces
    1 Tbs. + 1 tsp. salt
    1 Tbs. + 1 tsp. MSG (optional)
  1-3 green onions, minced
    1 large onion, thinly sliced
       cilantro to garnish

Heat skillet (NO OIL). Throw in the rice and stir vigorously until it changes color—to light yellow—being careful not to burn it. Remove from skillet and place in a soup pot with ½ gallon of water. Cook over medium heat until the rice thickens—it will appear overcooked. Add 1 tsp. salt and 1 tsp. MSG. Add water as needed to soup. While the soup is cooking, mix 1 Tbs. salt and 1 Tbs. MSG and rub on chicken pieces. Steam the chicken until it is cooked. Collect ½ cup of the drippings from the steamed chicken and pour into the rice soup. Shred the chicken pieces after they cool. Serve by pouring soup into bowls and adding layers of chicken pieces. Sprinkle in green onions and sliced onions. Lightly pepper to taste. Garnish with cilantro, bean sprouts, thinly sliced hot peppers, if desired.

Serves: 4-6.

NOTE: When I'm in a hurry and want a quick meal, I simply boil the chicken, constantly skimming off the foam that rises. When the broth remains clear, I add all the seasonings and cook until the chicken is fully done. Then I remove the chicken and add the raw rice. It must cook an additional 15-20 minutes. Thus, this meal can be ready within an hour.

Banh Canh
(Thick Noodle Pork Soup)

    1   package pork feet
    2   Tbs. chopped dry onions
    ½   tsp. MSG
    1   tsp. salt to taste
    1   Tbs. preserved cabbage
  2-3   Tbs. vegetable oil
    1   package *banh canh* (thick noodles)

Boil pork feet in a gallon of water until well done, 20-25 minutes. As foam rises to surface, skim it off to keep water clear. Heat the oil in a small skillet to very hot, remove from burner and place onions in the oil until they turn slightly yellow. Then pour this into soup. Add preserved cabbage and seasonings. Simmer for 30-45 minutes. Pour hot water over the *banh canh* to separate the noodles. Before serving, drop the noodles into the soup and cook 5-7 minutes. To serve: garnish with chopped onions, cilantro, and black pepper.

Serves: 4-6.

Bo Kho
(Sauteed Beef Soup)

1 lb. lean beef tips (or beef skirts), cubed
½ tsp. sesame oil
3 Tbs. soy sauce
2 green onions, finely chopped
2 medium potatoes, cubed
2 large carrots, chopped
1 small onion, sliced
3 Tbs. of chili powder
1½ tsp. crushed red peppers (adjust to taste)
2 tsp. salt
1 tsp. MSG

Mix the soy sauce and green onions; pour over beef and marinate for 30 minutes or longer. In the meantime, prepare the vegetables for cooking; set these aside while you sautee the meat cubes lightly in sesame oil. Put the meat in a large pot with 2-3 quarts of water and bring to a hard boil. After cooking for ten minutes, add the seasonings and lower heat to medium. Cook for 5 more minutes and add the vegetables. Cook soup for 6-8 minutes (or until the vegetables are tender). Serve with hard-crusted French bread.

Serves: 4-6.

NOTE: Lac prepares this soup often on cold evenings, a delightful "warm-up."

Pho Bo Vo Vien
(Meatball Soup)

> 1 lb. very lean ground beef
> ½ package Alsa (or 1 Tbs. baking powder)
> 1 onion, finely chopped
> 1 tsp. black pepper
> 2 Tbs. potato starch
> 1 Tbs. fish sauce
> ½ tsp. MSG
> ½ tsp. sugar

Plus:

> 1 large pot of beef soup, Pho Bo (see page 80)

Mix all the ingredients in a large bowl. Knead until smooth. Then grind the mixture in a food processor until it has a heavy clay-like texture. Put it back in the bowl and refrigerate for at least 30 minutes. When soup is boiling vigorously, remove mixture from refrigerator and begin forming into small balls, about 1-1½" in diameter. Drop into boiling soup. When the balls float to the top, they are ready to eat—in the soup, over rice noodles, or separately as appetizers.

Yield: Approximately 30-40 meatballs.

Bun Reu
(Crab Noodle Soup)

¾ lb. crab meat
1 Tbs. salt
1 tsp. fish sauce
½ tsp. MSG
3 tomatoes, cubed
3 green onions, minced
1 medium onion, thinly sliced
1 bundle of (Vietnamese) spinach, shredded
¼ head of lettuce
1 Tbs. vegetable oil
2 eggs
1½ tsp. black pepper
1 package of rice noodles, steamed and drained 15 minutes prior to serving

Mix crab meat with eggs, green onion, and black pepper. Coat the meat thoroughly. Bring ½ gallon of water to boil and add the salt, fish sauce, and MSG. Then put the coated crab meat into the boiling water for 10-15 minutes. During that time, stir-fry the tomatoes and onions, until the onions turn a light yellow. Pour the tomatoes, onions, and oil into the soup. To serve, fill bowls half full of noodles, topped with spinach pieces, green onions and lettuce. Then ladle soup into the bowl. Garnish with bean sprouts, hot peppers, and fresh lemon or lime juice.

Serves: 4-6.

Pho Bo
(Beef with Noodle Soup)

A point of interest: If you enter a "pho" restaurant (a Vietnamese transplant into many American cities), you may choose a regular bowl of this steaming broth; or, if you're a hearty eater, you may order *pho xe lua*, a bowl of pho "as big as a train!"

4-6 beef soup bones
  2 lb. (approx.) beef roast
  2 medium onions
  1 3-inch piece of gingerroot
  ⅓ cup star aniseed
  ½ tsp. MSG
  2 Tbs. salt (or to taste)
  ½ tsp. sugar
  3 green onions, chopped
    cilantro
  1 package Pho rice noodles, cooked and drained

Wash bones carefully. Boil them for 15-20 minutes in 1 gallon of water; then dispose of water. Wash bones again to keep the soup water clear. Refill soup pot, approximately 1-2 gallons of water. Bring to boil, then reduce heat to simmer for one hour. (Skim off beef foam as it appears.) As soup simmers, prepare other ingredients: Take gingerroot and whole onion and singe on high heat. the outside may be burned, but the juices should remain in them. Rinse off ginger and onion and put in the simmering soup. Add the aniseed. Stir in the seasonings and allow to simmer for 10-15 minutes more. Slice the roast *very* thin. To serve, increase heat until soup is very hot, even boiling. Half-fill soup bowls with Pho noodles, then place the thin slices of meat on top. Ladle the soup over the meat, and garnish with green onions and cilantro. Stir the soup to cook the meat slices. (If you prefer your meat well-done, pour approximately 2 cups of soup into a saucepan and drop the meat slivers into pan. Allow to cook to desired doneness.) Add bean sprouts, pepper slices, hoisin sauce if you like; or squeeze a small amount of fresh lime juice into soup.

Serves: 6-8.

NOTE: This recipe can be simplified if time is critical. Simply place the bones in a large pot of water and bring to a heavy boil. Skim the foam off the top as it rises. When the soup remains clear, approximately 30 minutes, add the rest of the seasonings. Simmer another 30-45 minutes while you prepare the noodles and meat slivers. Ready to serve!

Bun Bo Hue
(Hot and Spicy Soup)

  4-6 pork feet
1-1½ lb. of roast beef
  ½ tsp. meat tenderizer
  1-3 stems of lemon grass, cut into 3″ pieces
  1 Tbs. chili powder
  1 Tbs. vegetable oil
  1 tsp. chopped dry onion
1½ tsp. salt
  1 tsp. shrimp paste
  1 tsp. sugar
  1 tsp. MSG
  1 package rice vermicelli noodles, cooked and drained

Boil the pork feet 5-10 minutes; then drain. Cut the beef into bite-sized cubes, boil for 5-10 minutes, drain. In a deep saucepan half-filled with water, add pork feet and meat tenderizer. Cook over medium heat for 10-15 minutes Add the beef cubes and continue to cook over medium heat. In the meantime put oil in a small skillet, heat until very hot, remove from burner, and immediately throw in the chopped onion and chili powder. Stir well and pour into soup. Add the shrimp paste and seasonings to taste. Let soup simmer for 30-45 minutes, until pig's feet are well cooked. Soup is ready to serve. Fill bowls half full of rice noodles and ladle the soup over them. Serve with chopped green onion, cilantro, sliced peppers, and lime.

Serves: 4-6.

Hu Tieu
(Barbeque and Shrimp Soup)

```
 4-6  pork soup bones
   1  package (14 ounces) dried squid
   1  package (14 ounces) dried shrimp
   1  large onion, chopped
   2  Tbs. cooking oil
   1  Tbs. preserved cabbage
  ½  tsp. MSG
   1  Tbs. salt (or to taste)
  ½  tsp. sugar
   2  Tbs. sesame oil
12-16  fresh shrimp to fry
        thin slices of BBQ pork (Lac's Pork) (see p. 40)
   1  package of rice noodles, cooked and drained
        cilantro or parsley to garnish
```

Wash bones carefully. Boil bones in approximately 2 gallons of water for one hour. Skim the foam as it develops to keep the water clear. Rinse the dried squid and shrimp and add to the water. Boil for 30 minutes. In the meantime, heat the oil in a small skillet until very hot; remove from the heat and immediately toss in the onions. Stir quickly, but do not fry. As soon as the onions change color to a pale yellow, pour into the soup. Boil for 15 minutes, then add the seasonings. Prior to serving, stir in the sesame oil.

(continued)

Barbeque and Shrimp Soup — *(continued)*

Batter for Shrimp

To ½ cup of self-rising flour, add enough water to form a batter, 1-1½ cups. (Optional—for color, finely chop a green onion and stir into batter.) Clean shrimp, leaving on the tails. Holding shrimp by tails, dip into batter and deep fry until golden brown, approximately 2-3 minutes.

To serve, half-fill large soup bowls with noodles. Lay several pieces of pork on the noodle bed. Fill with soup broth. Place the fried shrimp in last. Garnish with cilantro, bean sprouts, thinly sliced hot peppers, if desired.

Serves: 6-8.

NOTE: This is one of my favorite soups, but it looks overwhelming to prepare. Thus, I suggest some shortcuts I have adopted when I don't have a full day to cook. The barbeque slivers can be bought . . . most Oriental restaurants and many groceries prepare this pork daily. And the shrimp can be added to the soup without being deep-fried in batter. Simply clean and boil for approximately 2 minutes.

Canh Chua Voi Ca
(Sweet and Sour Fish Soup)

  1 medium to large catfish
  1 cup fresh pineapple, cut into 1″ cubes
  2 small tomatoes, cut into 1″ cubes
  1 cup bean sprouts
  1 Tbs. vinegar
  1 Tbs. lemon juice
  1 tsp. oregano or crushed basil leaves
1-2 sliced hot peppers
  ¼ cup celery leaves
  ½ tsp. sugar
  1 Tbs. sesame oil

Clean the fish. Fill a large soup pot half-full of water, add vinegar and lemon. Bring to a vigorous boil. Add the fish and cook for approximately 15 minutes, until the fish is almost done. Add pineapple and tomato cubes. Return it to a boil; then reduce to medium heat. Then add the celery leaves, oregano or basil, bean sprouts, and peppers. Cook for 5 minutes. Add seasonings to produce the sweet and sour flavor. Finally stir in the sesame oil and serve.

Serves: 6-8.

Bun Moc
(Turkey Sausage and Pork Ball Noodle Soup)

1 lb. lean pork, cubed	½ tsp. sugar
1 lb. boneless turkey breast meat, cubed	2 tsp. potato starch
	2-3 green onions, minced
2½ tsp. Alsa powder	
6 tsp. fish sauce	1½ tsp. salt
1 tsp. MSG	aluminum foil, string

1 package of rice vermicelli noodles, cooked and drained before serving

Part I—Preparing the meat:

Mix the meat, Alsa, fish sauce, MSG, sugar, and potato starch; knead until smooth. Refrigerate for 10 minutes. Remove and grind the mixture in a food processor until it has a thick, clay-like consistency. Use ⅘ of the mixture for sausage and ⅕ for meatballs. To make the sausage, place the ⅘ portion in aluminum foil, creating a long tube-like roll. Tie the roll tightly and steam it for an hour.

Part II—Preparing the soup:

The soup is prepared exactly as the Pho Bo recipe (page 80); however, chicken soup bones are substituted. To serve: slice the sausage into ¼" slices. As the soup boils, form the remaining ⅕ into balls about 1-1½" in diameter and drop into the soup. When they rise to the surface, the soup is ready to eat. Place noodles in a bowl, ladle in soup, add strips of sausage and meatballs. Garnish as desired with green onions, bean sprouts, cilantro, and hot peppers.

Serves: 6-8.

Chao Long Heo
(Pick-a-Pork Soup)

      2 lb. pork heart, tongue and stomach
    1½ cups rice
      1 tsp. lemongrass, minced
      1 tsp. hot peppers, sliced
      1 tsp. black pepper pods
      1 Tbs. salt
      1 tsp. MSG
    1½ Tbs. fish sauce
      3 green onions, minced

Heat a small skillet, but use no oil. Throw in the rice and stir vigorously until it turns to a light yellow. Remove the rice from the skillet and place in a large saucepan with 4 cups of water. Add pork heart, tongue, and stomach, lemongrass, hot peppers, and pepper pods to the mixture and cook until the rice thickens. It will appear overcooked. Add salt, MSG, fish sauce, and water as needed; cook for another 7-10 minutes. Sprinkle green onions on top, and the soup is ready to serve. Bean sprouts, fresh lemon or lime juice, cilantro, and parsley add interesting flavors to this soup.

Serves: 4-6.

Chao Long Ga
(Liver and Rice Soup)

½ lb. boneless, skinless chicken breasts
1 lb. liver and gizzards
½ cup rice
½ cup mung beans
1½ tsp. salt
1 Tbs. fish sauce
1 medium onion, thinly sliced
1 tsp. sugar
3 Tbs. minced onion

Cut chicken breasts into small pieces and tenderize them with a mallet. Put chicken breasts, liver, gizzards, rice and mung beans in a large sauce pan with 5 cups of water. Boil rice and ingredients until the rice appears to be overcooked. Add salt, fish sauce, chopped onion, and sugar to the mixture and cook for 5-7 minutes. Sprinkle the minced green onions over the rice (to taste) and the soup is ready to serve. Garnish with bean sprouts, lime or lemon juice, sliced hot peppers, mint, or cilantro as desired.

Serves: 6-8.

Vit Tiem
(Duck Soup)

      1 duck, cleaned
      6 inches sugar cane, sliced into ½″ pieces
      2 Tbs. salt
      ½ tsp. sugar
      3 green onions, chopped
      ¼ tsp. MSG
      3 fresh garlic cloves
      1 can lotos seeds
 10-15 black mushrooms
      1 cup red wine

Boil duck and sugar cane in 1½ gallons of water for an hour. Add salt, sugar, onions, MSG, and garlic, then return to a boil for another 5-10 minutes. Add the lotos seeds and black mushrooms and boil for 5-10 minutes. Stir in the red wine. Soup is ready to serve. May be eaten with noodles or on rice.

Serves: 4-6.

Chao Vit
(Boiled Duck with Ginger Rice Soup)

1 5-6 lb. duck (including liver and giblets)
1 cup white rice
½ cup fish sauce
3 Tbs. minced fresh coriander leaves
3 Tbs. minced scallions
1 small head of romaine lettuce, separated
1 cucumber, peeled, seeded, shredded
1 bunch of fresh mint leaves
2 Tbs. gingerroot, peeled and shredded

In a large soup pot place the duck, the liver and the giblets with enough water to cover them. Bring to a hard boil, and simmer the mixture, skimming off the foam as it surfaces, for approximately 1 hour or until the duck is tender. Remove the duck, liver and giblets and put on a platter. Keep them covered loosely, warm. Skim the fat from the soup stock, set it aside, and boil over high heat until the stock is reduced to approximately 8 cups. Put 3 Tbs. of the fat skimmed from the soup into a skillet over a moderate heat. Add the rice, and cook, stirring constantly for 3 minutes, or until it becomes translucent. Pour rice into the stock, cover, and simmer for 20 minutes. Add fish sauce, coriander, salt and pepper, to taste, and keep the soup hot.

In the meantime prepare the duck for serving. Using a meat cleaver, chop it in half lengthwise; then chop off the legs and cut them into bite-sized pieces. Remove and discard the backbone and cut each half into small pieces. Thinly slice the liver and giblets and arrange on a large platter, decorated with romaine leaves, coriander, and mint.

Ladle the soup into large soup bowls. To serve: add slices of liver and giblets and gingerroot. Wrap the duck pieces in the romaine leaves along with the cucumber shreds and mint leaves. Dip in special sauce Nuoc Mam Gung (see p. 45).

Serves: 6-8.

Bun Thang
(Chicken Soup)

3-4 qts. chicken broth
1 large (4-5 lbs.) chicken, cut up
4-5 Tbs. fish sauce
¼ lb. chicken hearts or gizzards
1 Tbs. cooking oil
½ lb. bean sprouts
1 cup coriander sprigs
4 green onions, thinly sliced
¼ tsp. pepper
¼ minced cilantro
   prepared rice noodles
   egg strips (recipe on page 101)

In a large soup pot bring chicken broth to boiling. Add chicken to broth except for heart, gizzard, liver and breast. Cover and simmer for 25 minutes. Add breast, recover, and continue cooking until breast is done, approximately 20 minutes longer. Remove chicken and cool. Skim and discard fat from broth. Pull meat from chicken bones, discard skin and bones. Then shred chicken. Remove tough membranes from heart and gizzards, then cut these pieces into tiny strips. In a small frying pan, stir giblets in cooking oil over high heat until lightly browned, approximately one minute. Stir in 2 Tbs. fish sauce. To serve: each individual will select from the following to fill a large soup bowl — chicken, giblets, bean sprouts, noodles, egg strips, nuoc mam, cilantro, and green onions. After the portions have been placed in each of 6-8 bowls, the hot broth will be ladled over them.

V
The Little Ninja

For many months after my marriage I felt like an outsider to the Vietnamese community. Not that I was treated badly. Much to the contrary. The interactions among my adopted family were casual, bantering. Although I was treated with great deference and respect, it was obvious that I was "different." I was never teased or jokingly chastised. Special foods were selected and prepared for me. Conversations were halted in mid-stream so that someone could painstakingly explain in English what was being said. I was never allowed to help in the kitchen. In effect, I was treated as an honored guest, not as a family member.

I can pinpoint the exact day when all of this formality was to be changed: February 14, 1981, the date I announced my pregnancy.

Both Ma and Ba had been eagerly anticipating that announcement from the day we returned from Acapulco. Seldom did we visit them that Ma failed to stress, with a significant arch of an eyebrow, each new birth in the Vietnamese community. As the months plodded by with no heir apparent, they had begun to despair of ever becoming *Ba Noi* and *Ong Noi*, the names by which their son's children would traditionally address them. (Their daughter's children, in contrast, would call them *Ba Ngoai* and *Ong Ngoai*, which indicate they are "outside" the family, for they bear another name.)

So my Valentine's Day gift was greeted with great jubilation. I entered a special world then: I carried the grandson who would serve the ancestral spirits after Ma's and Ba's deaths. That I would deliver a girl-child was never even considered; not only had my wedding experience foretold a male firstborn, but Ba, sort of a seer within the community, had ordained a grandson. That year, with some twenty birth predictions to his credit, he was incorrect only once, and then he was working from invalid data, he contends.

Ba knew. Indeed, he did. But just to confirm his initial prediction, he performed two other diagnostic tests. The first involved pencil and paper, mathematical determination, and an elaborate Oriental secret formula, which I take to be something like this: First, add the ages of the two parents; subtract the circumference of the mother's waist at the full moon during the third month; then multiply by the square root of the distance from San Antonio to Vietnam as measured in Burmese furlongs. Voila! A boy!

The second test proved simpler.

After the second trimester, its validity, according to Ba, is indisputable. My Vietnamese version of sonargram took place one summer afternoon as we were leaving Ba's home. As I was almost out the door, Ba abruptly called out, "Chi Hai!"

Startled, I turned to respond, "Sir?"

At that, Ba and his several cronies cackled in delight. I had turned to the left, the correct direction to designate a male child. (I have no doubt that had I turned to the right, Ba would have claimed invalid data.)

With this pregnancy, I "became" Vietnamese. Ma clucked over me, attempting to ease my minor discomforts and gently chiding me when I failed to eat what she considered appropriate foods. If she had been diligent in cooking for Lac and me during the prior two years, she became fanatic after Valentine's Day. Counting calories and weight watching for pregnant women are unheard of among the Vietnamese. This, I realized, was a splendid tradition. I entered a six months' feeding frenzy, broken only by trips to the obstetrician, who had herself developed a taste for Vietnamese cuisine.

Unlike many Americans, I had learned to enjoy the sharp taste of *o qua*, or bittermelon, a Vietnamese source of prenatal vitamins. If a week passed without our visiting Ma, she picked several *o qua* from her backyard garden, stuffed them with meats and rice threads, and wended her way to our house, which by that time was twenty miles across town.

It was during just such a visit that the rumblings of a problem developed. Cultural, of course.

Through careful financial maneuvering, shrewd negotiating and boldfaced misrepresenting of assets, Lac and I had managed to qualify (barely) for our first home loan soon after learning of my pregnancy. We pressed for a quick closing, fearing that a potential loss of my income would thwart our plans, and we moved into our roomy new home. The furniture we salvaged from our apartment could, by a discerning decorator, be classed as Early Hideous: it was truly shabby in our new home. Our couch, faded and worn, seated three in discomfort, and a matching armchair completed our suite.

That afternoon Ma, Ba, and their guests from Houston, Mr. and Mrs. Phat, were seated on our pathetic furniture and by default, Lac landed on the floor. Conversation hummed, as I prepared refreshments for our guests. After serving them, I chose the only remaining space to join the circle, the hearth of the fireplace. No sooner had I settled myself there, then Ba commanded, "Move, Chi Hai! Don't sit there!"

With barely a moment's hesitation, I slid from my

perch to the floor. Confused, I looked toward Lac, who merely grinned and shook his head slightly. My in-laws and their guests talked quietly among themselves for several minutes, while I pondered what gaffe I had committed *this* time. Finally, Ba explained, "*Ong Tao*, spirit of the fire, demands respect. You must not sit on his fireplace; he could take your baby!"

Though my beliefs do not at present include *Ong Tao*, I make it a point never to dishonor him in Ba's presence.

Later that evening while discussing my breach of etiquette with Lac, I learned another interesting point that pregnant Vietnamese women must know. It is bad luck for a person to see either a cat or a pregnant woman the first thing in the morning. Should a pregnant woman be the first sight on the *Tet*, or New Year, that is extremely bad luck for the coming year. In the villages of the countryside, the pregnant women would customarily refrain from shopping until afternoon to

assure that the shopkeepers weren't faced with them as their first customers. (Okay, I agreed, no hearth-sitting for this Mama, but nothing short of major calamity could keep me out of the malls, pregnant or otherwise!)

As a suddenly precious, pampered one, I waddled serenely through an uneventful pregnancy. Oh yes, there was one man who inquired, with typical Vietnamese bluntness, how much weight I had gained. (His wife, a Vietnamese doll the size of my thumb, had gained 2½ pounds during her entire pregnancy.) By then I had learned how to counter such questions by the simple expedient of feigning deafness.

I told myself that I was thoroughly happy and contented with carrying this tiny ninja-child, the nickname our dojo family had given to the infant so ticklish he would try to "hide" from a hand laid on my stomach. Yet privately I feared complications in the delivery. I harbored a semi-superstitious fear that I didn't deserve this much happiness, that it would all be ripped from me at any moment.

In fact, the delivery proved easy, my recovery fast. My son was named Jason Lac to represent his ties to two cultures. The next morning after his birth I prepared to leave, certain that Dr. Wratten would agree when she saw me skipping down the hall with my new-born Ninja. Though she had signed me out before 10:00 a.m., I waited impatiently for Lac to return by noon with his mom, who, according to tradition, planned to carry her first grandchild home from the hospital. I had been initially disappointed that I wasn't going to be the one to carry Jason home, but when

I saw her standing there in specially made *ao dai*, glowing with anticipation, I knew that this is one tradition well worth honoring.

Too bad Big Nurse did not share my sentiments. In she bustled, the image of starched efficiency. "Time to dress this little man," she said. "Need some he'p gettin' 'im ready?"

"No thanks, I'm all packed. His little *gi* is right here; I'll dress him. You can run along and help someone else."

"No'm," she countered. "Hospital rules. I gotta tote this baby outta here."

"But my mother-in-law is here. She can take care of that for me. No need to bother."

By this time Ma sensed that all was not proceeding as per tradition. A hint of a crease furrowed her brow, and she stared at the nurse, who stood a good head and shoulders taller than she.

"Nope," Nurse repeated. "I gotta tote this baby. It's my job."

And I am sure Ma's thoughts would have translated, "I am here to tote this baby. It's my *tradition*."

So the two women continued to eye each other, taking the opponent's measure, one pulled by duty and responsibility, the other by millenia of custom.

"How about a compromise?" I suggested. "You carry him past the nursing stations, and Ma can carry him in the elevator and outside the door. That way, everyone is satisfied, no?"

Looking a bit dubious, Big Nurse conceded, "Yeah, I guess so, but y' know . . . " As she finished her sentence, I joined in on the chorus, "I gotta tote that baby."

The absurdity of the situation was finally manifest, and we all erupted into laughter. Thus, both Ma and the Big Nurse "toted" Jason from the hospital to our car. In a final transfer of the infant, Big Nurse laid Jason in Lac's arms, and he handed over the bundle to Ma who now awaited him in the back seat.

We were off to introduce Jason to his new home, new life, new family, for many of our karate family had gathered at our home. Regally as a queen in a coronation, Ma marched to the bassinet she had carefully prepared and placed Jason Lac in it.

With that tradition complete, she immediately began preparing for *Dau Thang*, a celebration of thanksgiving that occurs thirty days after a baby's birth. In it the spirits are blessed for allowing the child to live. The Buddhists believe that the baby is a gift from the spirits, who may reconsider their present at any time within the first month and reclaim the child. When they choose not to do so, the family offers thanks and sacrifice on the family altar.

As always the altar is carefully prepared to display respect for the spirits. Incense is lighted, food and drink are spread for the "spirit-guests," and a special door is opened to invite them to enter. No one is allowed to eat or drink while the incense is burning, nor is anyone supposed to enter through the "spirit-door." (I learned that taboo the hard way, when once I followed my rather irreverent husband into the house through this entrance!)

After Ba and Ma burned the incense for Jason, they prepared to offer the finest gift to the spirits: Jason's hair. Normally it would have all been cut off and placed on the altar. Having seen a friend's baby immediately after her *Dau Thang*, I determined that my baby was not going to be bald—not even to appease the spirits! Ma, however, was equally determined (and had apparently learned the value of compromise in the Big Nurse episode). She snipped a two-inch piece of hair from the back of the baby's neck, then combed the rest over the bald spot, which I found two days later. Throughout all of this, as well as the commotion of thirty guests, the tiny guest of honor snoozed soundly, oblivious to the attention he was generating.

Not so his *Thoi Noi*, or "leaving the cradle" ceremony. At twelve months the babies are once again feted. The major significance of this event is that their futures are supposedly determined. After the incense burns down and appropriate prayers are chanted, the selection process occurs. Several symbolic items are placed on a tray: a clod of earth, a rice ball, a book, a ruler, a compass, among others. The baby, after dedication to the spirits, is allowed to select one symbol which represents his future. Eagerly Ma held the tray for Jason to survey, as everyone gathered around him. Without a moment's hesitation he chose his fate. Of course, the dirt ball. Definitely not a good symbol, for he had chosen the life of a farmer, a very hard existence in Vietnam. And to compound the decision, before Ma could remove the tray, he grabbed the rice ball, symbolic of the peasant class, as well. This bad omen so disappointed both Ma and Ba that, for them, the delight of the celebration was ruined. Not even my point that owning a 10,000-acre rice farm would not be so bad a future for my son managed to lighten their sorrow.

The *Thoi Noi* is the last celebration of age for the Vietnamese until they reach 60 years old. (Unless you count my young sisters-in-law who got with American traditions early, claiming birthdays three or four times a year). The sixtieth anniversary—called *Luc Tuan*—calls for the grandest of celebrations, for this age indicates that one has gained wisdom and maturity. Ba has already mentioned that he expects us to rent a large ballroom to celebrate his "coming of age." No doubt he has been planning the menu and the guest list for the past decade, at least!

Traditional Favorites

1. Boiled Crab Claws *(Cang Cua Luot)*
2. Steamed Pork and Shrimp Rice Cake *(Banh Beo)*
3. Squash Soup *(Canh Bi Dao)*
4. Steamed Duck with Ginger *(Ga Hap Gung)*
5. Sour Fish with Vegetables *(Canh Ca Chua)*
6. Fish Sausage *(Cha Ca)*
7. Shrimp Stuffed in Green Peppers *(Tom Ot Xanh)*
8. Sweet Rice and Mung Bean Rolls *(Xoi Cuc)*
9. Sauteed Beef Lemongrass *(Bo Uop Xa)*
10. Beef Fondue with Vinegar *(Bo Nhung Giam)*
11. Sour Meat Rolls *(Nem Chua)*
12. Chicken Curry *(Ca Ri Ga)*
13. Shrimp in Red Sauce *(Tom Ham)*
14. Shrimp Crepes *(Banh Xeo)*

Cang Cua Luot
(Boiled Crab Claws)

6-8 large crab claws, cleaned
1 package shrimp and crab boil
1 lemon, chopped into wedges
1 large onion, cut into fourths

In a large pot bring 1 gallon of water to a hard boil. Add the crab boil mix, lemon and onion. Allow to boil for 15-20 minutes before adding the claws. then drop in the crab claws and return to a full boil for 7-8 minutes. Drain and serve with fish sauce.

Serves: 4.

Banh Beo
(Steamed Pork and Shrimp Rice Cake)

  1 cup rice flour
  3 cups water
  ¼ lb. dried shrimp
  ¼ lb. lean pork

Thoroughly mix the flour with the water. Fill small cupcake tins approximately half-full. Steam these cups in a steamer for approximately 30 minutes, until the "cakes" are done. In the meantime, using a mortar and pestle (if available), mash the shrimp into powder form. Boil the pork until very done (approximately 25 minutes); then chop it into small pieces. Mix the pork with the ground shrimp and sprinkle over the top of the "cake." Dip in fish sauce.

Yield: 12.

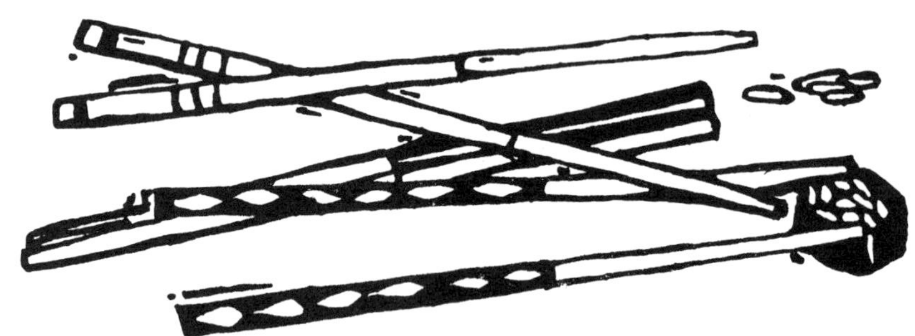

Canh Bi Dao
(Squash Soup)

    1 medium green squash ("Chinese squash")
    1 lb. fresh shrimp, cleaned and deveined
    2 green onions, chopped
    1 Tbs. vegetable oil
    ½ Tbs. fish sauce (or salt)
    ½ tsp. sugar
      egg strips

Cut squash into 3″ by ¼″ rectangular strips. Fill a medium saucepan ½ full of water and bring to a vigorous boil. Add shrimp; reduce heat to medium and boil for 2½-3 minutes, removing any foam as it accumulates. Add squash strips and cook for two minutes. Stir in fish sauce (or salt) and sugar, to taste. Add the chopped onion and vegetable oil; bring to boil again, cook three minutes at high heat. May be served alone or over rice, garnished with the egg strips.

Serves: 4-6.

Egg Strips

Beat 2 eggs with one Tbs. water. Coat a small non-stick frying pan with 1-2 tsp. cooking oil, including the sides. Then heat over medium low flame. When pan is hot, pour in ¼ cup of egg mixture, then quickly tilt pan to coat the bottom evenly. Cook only until egg feels dry on top, then turn onto a paper towel. Repeat process until mixture is used up. Cut the egg cakes into ¼″ wide strips. (An interesting variation on these strips is to add finely chopped green onions or mushrooms to the batter before frying.)

Ga Hap Gung
(Steamed Duck with Ginger)

6-8 black mushrooms (soaked for 10 minutes), or 8 oz. regular mushrooms
1 3-4 lb. duck
1 4-5″ stalk of ginger, thinly sliced
4 green onions, finely chopped
4 Tbs. fish sauce
1 Tbs. wine vinegar
½ cup raw peanuts
  pinch of cilantro
1 4″ stalk of lemongrass

Chop the mushrooms into fourths. Cut the meat from the duck, discarding the fat. Slice the giblets thinly. Place the meat, giblets, and mushrooms into a large casserole dish, then add ginger and onions. Crush and chop lemongrass, add the remainder of the ingredients, and mix very well to make sure the meat is thoroughly coated. Allow to marinate for 2-3 hours. Then place the casserole dish in the top part of a steamer, with water in the bottom. Bring to a heavy boil. Allow to steam on medium high heat for 30-40 minutes or until meat is just done. Excellent with rice, in soup, or dipped into fish sauce.

Serves: 6-8.

Canh Ca Chua
(Sour Fish with Vegetables)

    1   large catfish
    ¼   fresh pineapple
    2   stalks of celery, thinly sliced
    2   tomatoes, cut into small wedges
    ½   cup bean sprouts
    2   Tbs. mint leaves (or oregano leaves)
    1   tsp. fish sauce
    ½   tsp. salt
    2   tsp. vinegar
    5   cups water
    1   tsp. sugar
    3   hot peppers, thinly sliced

Clean fish. Cut into 2″ pieces diagonally across its body. Cut the pineapple into 1″ cubes. Bring water to a heavy boil in a large soup pot. Add vinegar, then the fish pieces. Cook the fish 4-5 minutes, then drop the pineapple cubes into the soup. Cook for an additional 5 minutes. Finally add in the remaining ingredients and bring mixture to a hard boil once again. Serve over steamed rice.

Serves: 4.

Cha Ca
(Fish Sausage)

1 large catfish, filleted
½ tsp. MSG
½ tsp. pepper
½ tsp. garlic powder
1 medium onion, thinly sliced
1 tsp. Alsa (or may substitute 1 tsp. baking powder)
1 tsp. potato starch
2 tsp. fish sauce

Clean the fish, making certain that no bones remain in the meat. (Yield should be approximately 1 lb. of meat.) In a large mixing bowl, mix all of the ingredients thoroughly. Then place the mixture in a blender and blend until there is a clay-like consistency. Return the mixture to a bowl, cover, and refrigerate for 2 hours. To serve, form the mixture into patties and fry as you would a hamburger.

Yields: 4-6 patties.

Tom Ot Xanh
(Shrimp Stuffed in Green Peppers)

1-1½ lb. shrimp, cleaned and deveined
  6 medium green peppers
  1 small onion, chopped fine
  2 tsp. salt
  ½ tsp. salt
  1 tsp. garlic powder
  1 tsp. potato starch
  ½ cup cooked bean threads (or rice vermicelli),
     drained
  1 Tbs. gingerroot, thinly sliced

Cut the tops off the green peppers and clean out the seeds, rinsing with clear water. Grind the shrimp, then add the remaining ingredients and mix well. Stuff the mixture into the peppers. Then steam for 30-40 minutes. To serve, top with bottled oyster sauce to taste.

Yield: 6.

Xoi Cuc
(Sweet Rice and Mung Bean Rolls)

2 cups sweet rice
1 cup rice flour
¼ cup water
½ cup mung beans
1 tsp. vegetable oil
1 tsp. green onions, chopped

Cover the mung beans with water and soak for 30 minutes. Cover the rice with water and soak for two hours. Mix the water with the rice flour to form a dough. Knead lightly 1-2 minutes and set aside. Heat the oil in a skillet over medium heat, then drain the water from the mung beans. Stir-fry the beans and onions in the oil for 5-10 minutes. Allow to cool. Using a mortar and pestle, if available, grind the bean-onion mixture into a powder. Now divide the dough into quarters and spread out on a flat surface to about ¼″ thickness. (You may spread by hand or with a rolling pin if you prefer.) Put a layer of the bean mixture onto this dough "shell," and fold it over to form a "sandwich" effect. Repeat process with the remaining dough quarters. In a steamer place a layer of sweet rice, then a layer of mung bean "sandwiches," alternating until the sandwiches are all placed in the steamer. End on a rice layer. Steam for 30-40 minutes.

Serves: 6-8.

Bo Uop Xa
(Sauteed Beef Lemongrass)

1 lb. beef (sirloin or roast)
6 tsp. minced fresh lemongrass
4 Tbs. cooking oil
4 garlic cloves, mashed to a paste
4 tsp. fish sauce (or to taste)
6 Tbs. ground allspice
4 onions, shredded
1 tsp. sugar
4 Tbs. dry roasted peanuts

Slice beef thinly, across the grain. With the flat side of a cleaver, pound the beef lightly and combine it with the lemongrass (or peel), 2 Tbs. of oil, the garlic, 2 tsp. of fish sauce, and the allspice. Blend the mixture well. In a skillet heat the remaining oil and fish sauce over high heat; add the onions and saute them, stirring for 3 minutes or until they are golden brown. With a slotted spoon, transfer the onions to a plate. Then add the meat mixture to the skillet, sprinkle it with sugar, and saute it, stirring for 1-2 minutes, or until it is just cooked. Arrange the mixture on a large platter, top with the onions, sprinkle with the peanuts, and serve.

Serves: 4.

Bo Nhung Giam
(Beef Fondue with Vinegar)

NOTE: The celebration of the "seven jewels" is a special dinner composed of seven small courses—all made with beef. The first course, presented here, is a light Vietnamese version of beef fondue enhanced by vegetables, fruit, herbs, and a piquant sauce. This course is prepared well in advance and served at the table.

¼ cup each sugar, water, white distilled vinegar
1 3" piece of daikon, peeled (optional)
1 large carrot, peeled and cut into tiny sticks
1 lb. beef eye of round, trimmed
1 large head of red tip lettuce, washed
1 small cucumber, cut into tiny sticks
1 large tart green apple
1 cup fresh mint sprigs
1 cup fresh cilantro
  Dipping sauce (see recipe below)
  cooking broth (see recipe below)
30-40 pieces edible rice paper (6-8" in diameter)

In a mixing bowl, stir together sugar, vinegar, and water until the sugar dissolves. If daikon is used, slice very thinly crosswise and place with carrot sticks into the vinegar mixture. Cover and refrigerate, stirring occasionally, for 1-4 hours. Cut apple into thin sticks and dip into lemon or lime juice.

In the meantime, slice beef as thin as possible (across the grain) and prepare the beef platters by arranging the slices in overlapping layers. Drain daikon and carrots. On separate plates, pile daikon, carrots, lettuce, cucumbers, apple sticks, mint and coriander. To serve, pour dipping sauce into 6 small bowls. Place the boiling cooking broth on a portable burner and keep it simmering. Arrange the platters of food beside the burner. Using a spray bottle of water, lightly moisten both sides of 6 pieces of rice paper and place them on a tray (do not stack them; they will stick!) Let stand until they can be folded easily, 20-30 seconds. Next, place selected fruits and vegetables from the plates (according to preference) on the rice paper. With chopsticks, drop a slice of meat into the simmering broth and cook until it loses its pinkness. Lift out meat and place on top of the vegetables. Fold bottom up and sides in, and dip in the sauce before eating. Repeat the process as desired.

Cooking Broth

In a large saucepan, combine 3 cups white distilled vinegar, 3 cups of water, 3 tablespoons cooking oil, 1 tablespoon salt, 8 small pieces of fresh ginger, ½ small onion sliced thinly, and 3 green onions chopped into 1″ lengths.

Dipping Sauce

Mix 1 cup each water, fish sauce, white distilled vinegar, and sugar with ½ cup finely shredded carrot, 3 tablespoons lime juice, 5 teaspoons minced red chilies, and 6-8 garlic cloves, pressed.

Serves: 6.

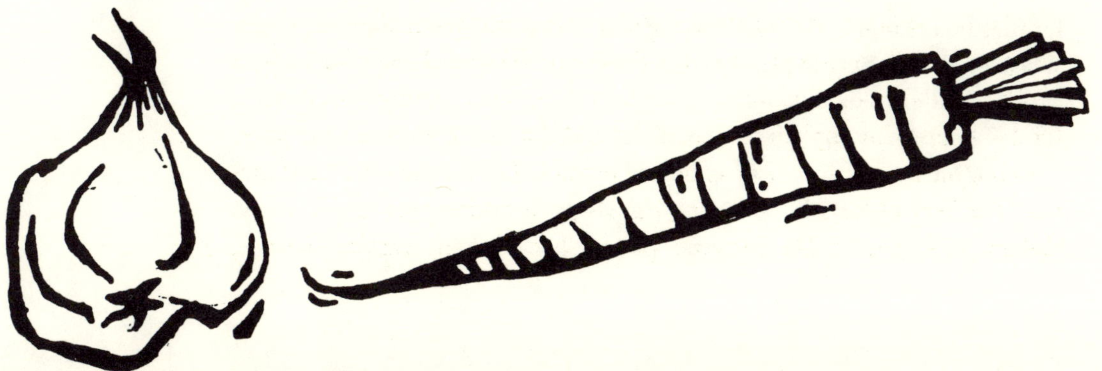

Nem Chua
(Sour Meat Rolls)

NOTE: This recipe is DEFINITELY not for everyone; however, it is a very popular treat in Vietnam.

  1 lb. lean pork butt
  1 lb. pork skin
  ¼ cup rice
  1 Tbs. cooking oil
  3 tsp. black pepper
 15 cloves fresh garlic
  1 tsp. meat tenderizer
  1 tsp. fish sauce

Boil pork skin till cooked; slice it into tiny strips. Cut the pork into thin slices; press to eliminate all juices, liquids in the meat. Heat the oil in a small skillet, then stir in the rice. Stir-fry the rice until it turns golden, approximately 3-4 minutes. Next grind the rice into a powder using a mortar and pestle if available. Mix the meats, the rice, with the seasonings in a large mixing bowl. Tear off two strips of aluminum foil, about 12-14 inches. Place the entire mixture on the doubled layer of foil, and roll it tightly into a sausage form. Let it stand at least 4 days. Then it may be eaten as is with fish sauce or it may be fried before serving.

Serves: 4.

Ca Ri Ga
(Chicken Curry)

2 Tbs. cooking oil
1 small onion, finely chopped
5 garlic cloves, minced
1 stalk fresh lemongrass, chopped
2 lb. chicken breasts, skinned and boned
3-4 medium sweet potatoes
3-4 carrots, thinly bias-sliced
½ cup water
2 tsp. brown sugar
2 tsp. curry powder
2 tsp. sesame oil
1 tsp. salt
¼ tsp. pepper
1 14-oz. can coconut milk
French bread slices or steamed rice

Cut chicken into bite-size cubes; peel and cut potatoes into thin strips. Set aside. Heat 1 Tbs. of cooking oil in a large skillet. Then add onion, garlic, and lemongrass (or peel) and saute for about 1 minute. Remove mixture from the skillet. Saute the chicken, half at a time, until tender, approximately 2-3 minutes. Remove the chicken and set aside. Heat the remaining oil in skillet and add sweet potatoes. Saute for 3-4 minutes until lightly browned. Then add carrots. In a small mixing bowl stir together the water, brown sugar, curry powder, sesame oil, salt, and pepper. Stir into the potato-carrot mixture in skillet. Bring mixture to a boil, then reduce heat. Simmer, covered, for 10-15 minutes or until vegetables are tender. Gently stir the onion mixture, chicken, and coconut milk into the vegetable mixture. Cook and stir over medium heat until heated through. Serve immediately with French bread slices or over steamed rice.

Serves: 4-6.

Tom Ham
(Shrimp in Red Sauce)

     1   lb. large shrimp, with shells and heads
     1   cup water
     ½   cup soy sauce
     1   Tbs. green onions, chopped
     1   tsp. chili powder
     ½   lime
     1   Tbs. cooking oil
     1   tsp. salt
     ½   tsp. MSG
     1   tsp. black pepper

Heat oil in a large skillet or wok. Put half of the onion in the pan and saute for 30 seconds. Carefully pour water and soy sauce into the pan, then add the washed shrimp. Cook and stir for 3 minutes. Add salt, MSG, and chili powder into the pan and cook for another 1-2 minutes, stirring constantly. Squeeze lime (or lemon) into the pan, continue cooking for 2 minutes. Sprinkle black pepper and the remaining green onion on top of the shrimp. Serve immediately with rice or French bread.

Serves: 4.

Banh Xeo
(Shrimp Crepes)

CREPE FILLING

4-6 medium Oriental dried mushrooms (**or** 8-10
   regular mushrooms)
 ½ lb. boneless pork
 ½ lb. medium shrimp
 1 small onion, chopped
 2 garlic cloves, minced
 1 tsp. cornstarch
 1 tsp. fish sauce
 1 cup water
   dash of salt, to taste
   dash of pepper, to taste

In a small bowl, mix the cornstarch, fish sauce, seasonings, and water. Set aside while you prepare the remainder of the filling. Thinly slice pork, about ½ x 2″. Then clean shrimp and cut in half lengthwise. Put 2 Tbs. of salad oil in a large pan over a high heat. Saute pork until meat is slightly brown, approximately 2 minutes. Add shrimp, onion, and garlic, stir until shrimp is pink and firm, another 2-3 minutes. Add mushrooms and corn-starch mixture. cook and stir until sauce thickens, continue cooking another 1-2 minutes. Keep warm.

(continued)

Shrimp Crepes — *(continued)*

CREPES

To prepare the crepe, lightly beat together 4 large eggs, one cup of water, dash of salt and pepper, to taste, and 3 Tbs. minced green onion. In a very hot skillet, add 1 Tbs. salad oil and heat. Then pour in enough of the egg mixture to barely cover the bottom of the pan and cook over a medium-high heat. (Adjust the temperature downward if the edges begin to burn before the middle cooks.) Lift the pan, gently shaking it to prevent the crepe from sticking. As the crepe begins to turn a light golden brown, spoon in the filling on one side. Fold the remainder over it, forming an omelette shape. Repeat the process until all of the mixture is gone. Makes 3-4 large crepes.

NOTE: The Vietnamese enjoy this dish by cutting small portions of the crepe and wrapping them in leaves of green leafy lettuce, then dipping them in fish sauce. It's a very messy ordeal the first time, but truly worth it!

VI
Earth Cakes & Moon Cakes

Like many Americans, whenever I had occasion to think of Buddhism, the image that came to mind was one of shaven-headed folks in airports or statues of cheerfully overweight men holding rice bowls. In a vague sort of way I once thought that this man was Buddha. I mentioned this to Lac, who quickly responded that he was in fact *Ong Dia*—the Earth god—a representation of prosperity.

Clearly my ignorance called for quick action if I were to advance in understanding of my new family. So, expecting enlightenment in six weeks or my money back, I read several articles on Buddhism, but these succeeded in leading me only to greater confusion. It appeared to be an Oriental "do-your-own-thing" philosophy. Pick a path, any path, to nirvana.

Of course, Lac was my first teacher. The other was my friend Elisa Gonzalez, a Catholic-Chicana-feminist-turned-Buddhist. A principle aspect of Buddhism is that the practitioner can select from among a broad spectrum of tenets, in the search for self-knowledge. Buddhists may even incorporate elements of other faiths into their life. Lac's family, for example, now includes the celebration of Christmas into their religious rituals.

My in-laws' traditions are Vietnamese and derive some of their attitudes from Zen philosophy, some from other, even less familiar (to me) sources. My family is not bound by the Buddhist caveat against eating meat, yet Ma undergoes a regimen of fasting for one month out of the year. During this time she declines to eat meats, eggs, and dairy products and relies instead on rice and vegetables she herself has grown. Once, during this month, I shuffled into her kitchen to offer help with preparing a family meal. Picking up a pair of chopsticks from the stove, I moved to stir the rice in the steamer. "Ah, no!" she shrieked, which I understood, followed by a swift torrent of Vietnamese. Lac explained that she had already stirred the soup bones with those sticks, and had I used them to stir the rice, it would have been contaminated for her.

Devotion to ancestors is central to the Vietnamese form of Buddhism, and the big familial celebrations of the year involve honoring the spirits of Lac's grandparents on the anniversaries of their deaths (*dam gio*). At first I thought it rather morbid to celebrate a relative's death, but have since learned how it meshes with the Buddhist belief in reincarnation. Death is seen as a victory, an opportunity for moving onward to a higher plane. The tone and spirit of Ma's celebrations are anything but depressing, and she is at her best when entertaining.

Once the meal is prepared for the living, Ma sets up a table before the family altar and lays out rice bowls, chopsticks, food, fruit, wine. There is a portion of everything that the family will eat. Then she lights three sticks of incense, bows thrice to the altar, and opens the door to invite the spirits to join our feast. No one may sample the food until the incense has burnt out—a span that gives the spirits ample time to enjoy their repast.

Finally, after outlasting what is surely the world's slowest incense, we get down to some serious eating. Ma frequently sets up tables for 15 to 20 people; she piles them end-to-end with wondrous Oriental delicacies. As a guest in many Vietnamese homes, I have discovered that their requirements for personal space contrast sharply with our American need to keep everyone at what we seem to think is a safe distance. Many a time I've shared a table I'd consider appropriate for four with ten to twelve Vietnamese, each person holding a bowl in one hand, chopsticks in the other. So long as there remains sufficient air-space for each guest to reach the table for second helpings, the feast progresses.

These personal holidays are significant in intimate ways that reaffirm the family as the nucleus of Vietnamese life and culture. But the public holidays, such as Buddha's birthday, *Tet* (the Lunar New Year), and *Tet Trung Thu* (a children's holiday), celebrate the national and cultural pride.

Phat To Giang Sanh, the celebration of the birthday of Buddha, is observed each year on the Sunday closest to the full moon in May. It is a day-time celebration marked by many multi-colored flowers decorating tables, altars, homes, and statues. In larger Vietnamese communities outside the homeland, floats bearing a statue of Buddha festooned with flowers wend throughout the streets, followed by dragon dancers and young girls wearing traditional *ao dai* and floral wreaths in their hair.

In these parades political banners wave alongside religious ones: "There Is No Religious Freedom in Vietnam" and "Long Live the Sacrificial Spirit of the Venerable Thich Quan Duc" (the first of many monks in Vietnam who burned themselves to death as protests). Other banners proclaim "Unity Is Strength" and "950 Million Buddhists All Over the World Unite With Other Religions to Serve World Peace." Most Vietnamese will attest that political concerns cannot be dissociated completely from their social, cultural, and religious life.

During this high holiday Ma offers special sacrifice to Buddha, who is referred to as the "Awakened One." She prepares the altar, presents food and drink in much the same way that she does for the ancestral spirits, then chants a series of prayers. Following these, Ma burns money in a vessel that has been blessed by a monk—fake money, that is. This particular tradition may have descended from a Chinese custom of destroying money to offer thanks to or beg indulgences of the spirit world. In any event, Ma reserves this ritual for only this most significant of celebrations.

The mid-autumn festival of *Tet Trung Thu* takes place at night during the full moon in October. This event was the first Vietnamese holiday relished by our son Jason, even though he had to wear *ao dai*, clearly not this three-year-old's idea of masculine attire.

Preparations for *Tet Trung Thu* may begin as much as two or three months before the date itself. Fathers and older siblings will begin making lanterns of bamboo and cellophane, in not one but many shapes—stars, fish, moons, animals. Mothers will sew new *ao dai* and will bake two types of special cakes for the evening ceremony: a flat, square one representing the earth, and a round, puffed one symbolic of the moon.

After these preparations, the children, dressed in new clothes and proudly bearing their lanterns, parade through the streets of the villages as the elders of the community watch. To emulate the rural customs, the Vietnamese here in America rent large party halls and even convention centers for these events. Jason recalls his first *Tet Trung Thu* vividly, for his lantern, a bumblebee in bright yellow and black, won first place in the judging.

And I remember that holiday with special fondness as well, for it marked my first "assignment" in the community at large. I was to recount the legend of *Chu Cuoi*, which warns all children to be obedient and to tell the truth. Knowing the keen devotion of the Vietnamese to their oral traditions, I was petrified that I might muddle my lines or, worse yet, go completely blank at the crucial time. But there was no graceful way out. This was more than a mere pageant—the community was entrusting me to carry out an important part of an observance that was to instruct their children in matters of behavior. (I purposely exposed myself to the Russian flu, only to contract it two days after *Trung Thu*.)

I studied and practiced with such concentration that I can recount the tale to this day . . .

"Chu Cuoi, a mischievous young rascal, delighted in weaving elaborate lies and in playing practical jokes on his companions. Though he meant to harm, his reputation for wit that was a little too quick and spirit a trifle too independent spread throughout the village.

"As a young man he was assigned—against the better judgment of many—the important task of guarding   Da, the sacred tree, from which came miraculous cures for every disease. The tree demanded honor and respect, but Chu Cuoi—such naughtiness—desecrated it by a thoughtless act.

"To his horror, the massive trunk began to tremble, the roots heaved themselves from the earth, and the tree surged toward heaven. Quickly Chu Cuoi grabbed the roots, attempting to hold fast the huge tree to earth, but he too was pulled upward—upward to the moon.

"There he sits still, under the mystical tree, longing for his home on Earth and the beloved wife he left behind."

Thus the earthcakes and the mooncakes both symbolize the reunion of the errant rascal with his wife, the spiritual ties between the earth and the moon. Lac says that historically the "mooncakes" also served as a means of clandestine communication among the politically oppressed peasants.

Tet, the celebration of the Lunar New Year, is the most important secular holiday for the Vietnamese and extends for two weeks usually during late January or early February. This holiday ushers in the New Year, which itself is a segment of the twelve-year lunar cycle that is probably most familiar to Westerners from paper placemats in Chinese restaurants. During that period Lac and I can really make no personal plans, for we know that Ma will be expecting us for several elaborate dinner parties.

At the first feast the youngsters will all attack their elders, demanding *"Lixi! Lixi!* Money! Money!" It is the custom that older people must present new money in bright red and gold envelopes to those who are younger. I pass out bunches of those little envelopes but receive only one, from Ma and Ba. Where cash flow is concerned, it seems, the custom of the culture do not extend to every branch of the family tree.

The spirit feast is celebrated during each of the parties of *Tet*, but other customs are equally important. One I dearly love is the injunction against house cleaning throughout the entire holiday. For two weeks, at least, I have a righteous excuse for, what my Mother so tactfully labels, my "cholera-infested" house.

Yet another custom is that each festive meal should be eaten with new utensils. Over the years my collection of two pairs of chopsticks, given to me as a wedding gift, has multiplied to 796 through this holiday tradition alone. What does one *do* with so many chopsticks? I suppose I could build a replica of the Temple of the Grand Shaolin in China with my collection.

Tet is traditionally a time of peace, for the Vietnamese believe that the way the year begins will predict its course. Since I first joined my Vietnamese family, I have been forbidden to wash dishes during the two weeks of *Tet* because of my tendency to drop things while drying them. A broken drinking glass, especially, would herald a terrible year.

Late in *Tet* there is a huge community gathering. Young people sing medleys of Vietnamese folk songs, occasionally interspersed with American rock and roll, while the elders dance. A fireworks display symbolizes the scaring away of a cruel dragon in mythology. The climax of the evening is a rousing costumed dance of the dragon, or lion, or—joy of joys—both!

The lion's head is massive, perhaps forty inches across the horns. The huge eyes, the size of bowling balls, can be made to wink and flutter by controls inside the mask. Vibrant reds and golds run riot in the color scheme of the head and continue on the train of fabric that composes the lion's body. To complete the ensemble, there are musical instruments: a barrel drum, a gong, and a set of brass cymbals. The lion stalks towards the circle of spectators, snapping its eyes and lolling its tongue, causing the young children to turn to their parents for reassurance. As the Lion advances, the crowd gives way, falling back a few steps, until the Lion dashes off to another quarter, and another, and another, teasing and pleasing the spectators.

Tet is indeed a glorious time for the Vietnamese. I have come to love this holiday and the spirit that it engenders. The night-feast of the full moon is the high point of the celebration. By tradition, special foods must be eaten at that very time to insure good fortune and prosperity.

No need for us to wait until *Tet* though. Why not include some of these special dishes during your own New Year celebration?

Festival Meals

1. Pickled Vegetables *(Dua Chua Bong Cai)*
2. Fried Pork with Tomato Sauce *(Heo Sot Ca)*
3. Shrimp Dumpling *(Banh Bot Loc)*
4. Sauteed Bamboo and Beef *(Bo Xao Mang)*
5. Fish with Black Bean Sauce *(Ca Chung)*
6. Octopus Stuffed with Pork *(Muc Don Thit Heo)*
7. Beef Lemongrass Shish-Ka-Bob *(Bo Nuong Xa Gung)*
8. Earth Cakes *(Banh Chung)*
9. Moon Cakes *(Banh Trung Thu)*
10. Phoenix Rolls *(Banh Phuong Hoang)*
11. Buns Stuffed with Meatballs *(Banh Pate)*
12. Sea Bass, Pineapple, and Bamboo Shoot Soup *(Canh Mang Chua Thom)*
13. "Steamboat" *(Lau Tom Thit)*
14. Dried Coconut Candy *(Muc Dua)*
15. Gingerroot Candy *(Muc Gung)*

Pickled Vegetables
(Dua Chua Bong Cai)

1   cup of vinegar
1   cauliflower
2   medium carrots
2   cups of sugar
1   Tbs. of salt
3   cups of water

Mix vinegar, water and salt together. Boil the mixture for 5-10 minutes. Chop carrots and cauliflower into small bites; put these pieces and the boiled mixture in a container and seal for three to four days. Rinse them with water before serving.

Serves: 6-8.

NOTE: A New Year's tradition among the Vietnamese is to pickle bean sprouts and green onions in the same fashion as the above vegetables. An easy recipe to prepare, these pickled vegetables add a delightful, unusual flavor to a meal.

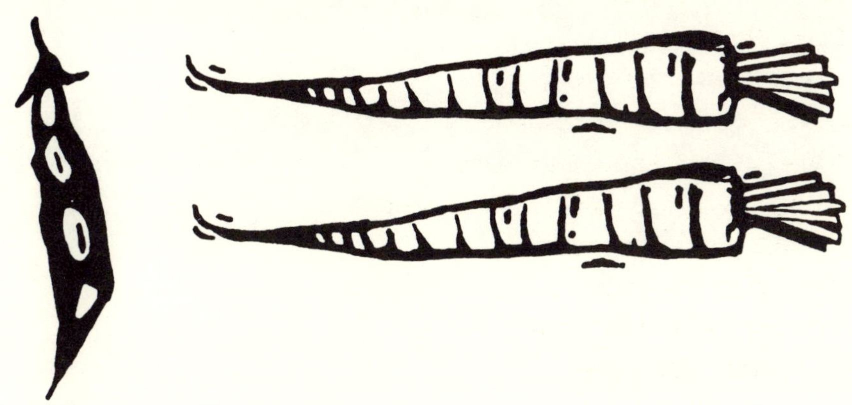

Heo Sot Ca
(Fried Pork with Tomato Sauce)

            1 Tbs. cooking oil
            2 lbs. pork chops, 1″ thick
            4 Tbs. fish sauce
            2 Tbs. soy sauce (optional)
            1 cup water
            4 Tbs. sugar
            1 Tbs. tomato paste
          2-3 garlic cloves, chopped

Heat oil in a large skillet over medium heat. Put the chops in the pan and cover. Brown one side, then turn and brown the other, keeping the skillet covered. When the pork is fully browned (about 30 minutes), prepare the sauce. In a mixing bowl, combine fish sauce, soy sauce, water, sugar, and tomato paste. Push all the pork chops to one side of the skillet, then put in the garlic. Brown lightly, and pour in the sauce mixture. Simmer, uncovered, for 10 minutes or until the sauce thickens. Remove the chops from the pan and slice across the grain into strips. To serve: put steamed rice on serving plates. Then lay the pork strips on the rice and pour remaining sauce over the entire dish.

Serves: 4-6.

Banh Bot Loc
(Shrimp Dumpling)

    1 cup rice flour
    ½ cup water
    ½ lb. cleaned shrimp
    ½ lb. lean ground beef
    ½ tsp. MSG
    1 Tbs. salt
    ½ tsp. black pepper

Mix flour and water to form a stiff dough. Chop shrimp in small pieces and mix with ground beef, salt, MSG, and pepper. Place the mixture in a blender and grind to a clay-like consistency. Roll out dough and cut into small circles, approximately 2″ in diameter. Place a teaspoonful of the shrimp mixture in the center of the dough, fold it in half forming a semicircle, and seal around the edges. Place the dumplings in a steamer and steam for 30-40 minutes. Serve with fish sauce.

Yield: 18.

Bo Xao Mang
(Sauteed Bamboo and Beef)

1 lb. lean round steak
2 green onions, finely chopped
2 Tbs. fish sauce
1 large can of bamboo shoots
   (or 2 cups fresh bamboo) thinly sliced
3 garlic cloves, crushed and minced
½ tsp. salt
   pepper to taste
½ cup water
2 tsp. cornstarch
   cooking oil

Cut the steak pieces against the grain into 3″ strips. Pour 2 Tsp. cooking oil in a skillet over high heat. Add beef and onions, saute briefly, for 1-2 minutes. Remove from skillet and add fish sauce. Stir well. Set aside. Add 3 more Tbs. of cooking oil to skillet and reheat. Saute bamboo shoots for approximately 1 minute. Add the garlic and continue to saute. Add salt and pepper. Immediately return beef to skillet and mix well. Mix the cornstarch and water until smooth. Then pour into skillet. Stirring constantly, cook about 30-45 seconds, until liquid is reduced slightly. Remove from heat. Serve over rice.

Serves: 4.

Ca Chung
(Fish with Black Bean Sauce)

2 large redfish
1 Tbs. black bean sauce
½ tsp. MSG
¼ cup dried black mushrooms
½ cup rice vermicelli noodles
1 medium onion, thinly sliced
1 Tbs. gingerroot, thinly sliced
1 hot pepper, thinly sliced on bias
¼ Tbs. salt
½ 8-oz. can coconut milk
1 tsp. black pepper

Clean fish and slash fish diagonally. Soak mushrooms in water for 10-15 minutes, then slice into small pieces. Cook and drain noodles. In the bottom of an oven-tempered glass casserole dish, place the black bean sauce, mushroom pieces, onion, gingerroot, hot peppers, and noodles. Spread evenly. Place the fish on top of this mixture. Pour the coconut milk, MSG and black pepper over the fish. Place uncovered casserole in a steamer and steam for 45 minutes Ready to serve.

Serves: 4.

Muc Don Thit Heo
(Octopus Stuffed with Pork)

      1 lb. lean ground pork
      ¼ package thin rice noodles
      4 black mushrooms
      ¼ tsp. salt
      1 tsp. black pepper
      1 Tbs. chopped green onion
      1 egg
    1-2 Tbs. cooking oil
      2 lb. octopus

Soak the black mushrooms in water for 10-15 minutes, then slice very thinly. Cook and drain noodles. In a small mixing bowl, thoroughly mix ground pork, noodles, mushroom slices, salt, pepper, green onion, and egg. Peel off outside skin of octopus. Rinse with clear water. then stuff the ground pork mixture into the body of the octopus; steam for 25 minutes. Next fry in very hot cooking oil for 6-8 minutes, turning often.

Serves: 4-6.

Bo Nuong Xa Gung
(Beef Lemongrass Shish-ka-Bob)

         1 lb. lean beef roast
        ½ Tbs. salt
         2 Tbs. fish sauce
         4 stalks lemongrass
       1½ tsp. black pepper, to taste
         1 Tbs. gingerroot, minced

Slice the beef into paper thin slices at least 3 x 4″. A butcher will often machine slice the roast for you. Cut off and dispose of the leafy part and the root of the lemongrass. With the side of a cleaver or large butcher knife, smash the remaining piece, then mince it. Mix lemongrass, ginger, fish sauce, salt, and pepper in blender. Blend for 5-10 seconds. Lay out beef slices and spread approximately 1/2 teaspoon of mixture onto the center of the beef strips. Fold and roll tightly into a ball, with the mixture inside the roll. Run skewer sticks through 3-5 rolls at a time. Barbeque over hot coals 5-8 minutes, at least until pink is gone.

Serves: 4.

Banh Chung
(Earth Cakes)

NOTE: The Earth Cakes are a very complicated recipe; however, because of their importance to the Vietnamese during their most important secular holiday, I have enjoyed experimenting with them. And failing. Perhaps you might like the challenge of the Earth Cakes to help assure a happy, fortune-filled year.

12 oz. of hulled mung beans
7 cups of sweet rice
6 scallions
¼ cup of fish sauce
½ tsp. pepper, or to taste
2 lbs. lean pork roast, cut in 2″ cubes

Soak mung beans and sweet rice separately overnight. Drain and allow them to dry in separate colanders or on towels for 2-3 hours. In the meantime, mash the scallions and add the fish sauce and pepper. Add this mixture to the pork; marinate for 2 hours.

The Vietnamese prefer banana leaves for wrapping these cakes; however, if they are unavailable, you may use aluminum foil (doubled) as a handy alternate, or the type of corn husks used in making tamales. Tear off fourteen pieces of the wide foil, approximately 12″ long. Double for wrapping. Then cut 8 pieces of strong cord at least 50″ long. Now begin forming the cakes on either the large leaves of the banana plant or on the foil. In the center form a 5″ square of the rice. On top of that, place ¼ cup of mung beans in a 4″ square. Next a piece of pork, then another ¼ cup of mung beans and another cup of rice. As you continue with the layers, your ingredients begin to take on a pyramid shape.

Earth Cakes — *(continued)*

Fold the foil over length-wise and seal carefully. Then seal one end of the container, leaving the other open. Drop in more rice to cover than end, then seal. Package looks like a tightly wrapped square meat loaf. Open the opposite end to add more rice there. Your final results should be a central piece of meat surrounded by a layer of mung beans, which itself is surrounded by the rice. For added assurance before cooking, wrap the bundles in foil again. Wrap the string around the package several times around both the length and the width. Continue forming these cakes until the mixture is all gone.

Place the cakes in cold water. Bring to a boil. Boil for six hours, adding water as needed to keep the cakes covered. Next remove from water, cool and refrigerate. Cakes will last for several weeks and can be reheated in oven.

Yield: 6 cakes.

Banh Trung Thu
(Moon Cakes)

1 cup of cooked mung beans
1 "1000-year-old" egg (Chinese duck egg, available
   in Oriental markets)
1 cup of flour
1 stick of butter
1 pinch of crushed roasted peanuts
¼ tsp. of crushed lotos seeds, sauteed
½ cup vegetable shortening
½ cup ice water

Whip together shortening and ice water. Add flour to form a sticky dough. Bounce around on a floured board until you get the right consistency. Roll out dough to approximately ¼" thickness. Cut into 4 x 4" squares. Mash hulled mung beans into paste and spread over squares. Peel egg and discard the white. Chop up the yellow and sprinkle pieces of it, the peanuts, and the lotos seeds on top of the mung paste. Wrap or fold the dough to form either a circle of a square around the mixture. Press in tightly to form a firm shape. Spread butter on a baking pan such as a layer cake pan. Bake at 400° for 20-25 minutes or until crust is brown.

Yield: 6 cakes.

Banh Phuong Hoang
(Phoenix Rolls)

2	filleted chicken breasts
10	strips of ham, approximately 2" x ½"
12-15	small shrimp, peeled and deveined
2	tsp. green onions, minced
2	tsp. lemongrass, minced (optional)
½	tsp. salt
¼	tsp. pepper, to taste
	cornstarch
1	cup cooking oil

Slice the breast fillets into very thin strips, about five pieces per breast. Flatten with the edge of a knife or cleaver. Mash the shrimp in a small bowl or in a blender. Then add the onions, lemongrass, salt and pepper, and continue to blend until the result is a thick paste. To fill the rolls, lay the filleted pieces on a cutting board and place a ham strip on the narrower edge. On top of the ham, add a teaspoon of the shrimp mixture. roll the chicken tightly over the filling. If necessary, run a thin skewer stick through the entire roll to keep it together. Finally dip each roll in cornstarch, coating it completely, and deep fry until a golden brown. Drain and serve with spicy fish sauce.

Yield: 10 rolls.

NOTE: Larger rolls can be made as a main course.

Banh Pate
(Buns Stuffed with Meatballs)

MEATBALLS	BUNS
½ lb. lean ground pork	¼ cup milk, scalded
1 tsp. salt	2 tsp. butter
½ tsp. pepper	½ tsp. sugar
1 tsp. MSG (optional)	½ tsp. salt
1 Tbs. fish sauce	1 packet yeast
1 tsp. garlic powder	1-1½ cups flour

Prepare the dough for buns. Scald the milk. Add butter, sugar, salt. Dissolve yeast in ⅓ cup of very warm water. When milk has cooled to lukewarm, add the yeast. Stir in the flour and knead for 3-5 minutes to form a soft ball. Allow to rise to double, approximately 1-2 hours.

In the meantime prepare the meatballs by mixing all the ingredients thoroughly. Then form into balls approximately 2″ in diameter. After the dough has risen, punch down, and begin forming the buns. Break off a piece of dough about 3-4″ in diameter. Roll out, place a meatball in the middle, and then seal the bun around the meatball. Continue this process until all buns are formed. Bake at 350″ on a lightly greased cookie sheet for 20-25 minutes, or until the buns are a crispy, golden brown.

Yield: 12 buns.

HINT: I have modified this recipe a bit to suit my taste for well-cooked meat. Before forming meatballs, I lightly saute the pork, then add the seasonings. At that point the meat will not hold together in balls, so I simply spoon the mixture onto the dough and form into buns.

Canh Mang Chua Thom
(Sea Bass, Pineapple, and Bamboo Shoot Soup)

2 oz. lump tamarind
1 8-oz. can of whole bamboo shoots, drained
½ pineapple, peeled and cored
2 Tbs. peanut oil
1 Tbs. sugar
2 sea bass fillets, 4-5 oz. each
2 Tbs. fish sauce
1 Tbs. minced fresh mint leaves (or 1 tsp. dried)

Cut pineapple into 1 x ½″ pieces. Skin and cut fish fillets into 1″ pieces. Set aside. In a small metal bowl, pour ¼ cup boiling water over the tamarind; let stand for 5 minutes or until tamarind is soft. Then press the tamarind through a fine sieve into a bowl. Set aside. Blanch the bamboo shoots in a sauce pan of boiling water for 1 minute. Drain the shoots in a colander, rinse with cold water, then slice them crosswise. Next saute the bamboo shoots and the pineapple in 1 Tbs. of the peanut oil over medium high heat for 1 minute. Transfer the mixture to a bowl and sprinkle the sugar over it. Boil 4 cups of water and then add the sea bass fillets. Cook for 1 minute. Add the tamarind, fish sauce, and mint, and bring to a hard boil. Serve in large bowls and float ¼ tsp. of remaining peanut oil on the surface of each serving.

Serves: 6.

Lau Tom Thit
("Steamboat")

*NOTE: The "Steamboat" is more than just a meal, it is an event. I first partici-
pated in this unique cultural experience during a brief trip to the West Coast.
There Lac and I visited Mr. and Mrs. The (pronounced Tay), who had been on
the same boat with Lac when he escaped from Vietnam. As Mrs. The declared,
"When 'steamboat' floats, conversation floats too!"*

SOUP INGREDIENTS

  2 stalks lemongrass
  4 cloves of garlic
  2 Tbs. gingerroot
  1 medium to large onion
  1 tsp. MSG
  2 Tbs. fish sauce
  1 tsp. salt
  4 serrano peppers
4-5 bay leaves
  1 Tbs. cooking oil
     water
  1 16-oz. package rice vermicelli

VEGETABLES/MEATS

½ lb. mushrooms
½ broccoli bunch
1 cup cauliflower florets

Steamboat — *(continued)*

6 okra spears
1 lb. shrimp
1 lb. lean beef

(Other options could include octopus, scallops, lobster, crab, pork, chicken — in essence, any meats or vegetables you choose!)

GARNISHES

½ lb. bean sprouts
1 bunch cilantro, chopped
2 serrano peppers, thinly sliced
4-6 lime wedges
½ head lettuce, separated

To prepare the soup, cut the lemongrass into 2″ pieces, then slice those pieces in half lengthwise. Smash and mince the garlic cloves, and slice the gingerroot very thinly. Cut the onion in half, one half to be sliced thinly for garnishing, the other half to be chopped for the soup. Next, cut the lime in half, one half to be sliced thinly, the other to be cut in wedges for garnishing. In a large electric wok, heat the cooking oil to 400°. Add the lemongrass, garlic, gingerroot, and the chopped onion. Stir-fry until the garlic turns brown, then carefully fill the wok approximately ¾ full with water. Add MSG, salt, lime slices, serranos, and bay leaves. Occasionally stirring the soup, boil it for 15-20 minutes while you prepare the other ingredients.

Ingredients to be cooked in soup:

Drop noodles in boiling water and cook 3-5 minutes, until soft. Don't overcook! Drain in colander, set aside. Clean and devein the shrimp. Slice the beef paper thin. (If you choose other meats, cut them into bite-sized chunks.) Layer all meats attractively on a large serving platter. Clean vegetables and prepare by cutting mushrooms in half, washing the broccoli and cauliflower, and chopping the okra diagonally into 1″ pieces. Place the prepared vegetables on another serving platter.

To serve:

Guests eat from rice bowls with chopsticks. Place the wok in the center of the table, surrounded by the platters of meats, vegetables, and garnishes. Guests select their foods, drop them into the boiling soup, and allow to cook to taste. In the meantime, they will fill their bowls with rice noodles and preferred garnishes.

Additional Note: Though the process seems lengthy—and indeed is time-consuming—it is a wonderful dish for entertaining. (By sharing the tasks, Lac and I have managed to cut the preparation time down to 90 minutes, and who spends less than that when preparing for a dinner party?) Also the soup may be refrigerated and used again with no loss of flavor.

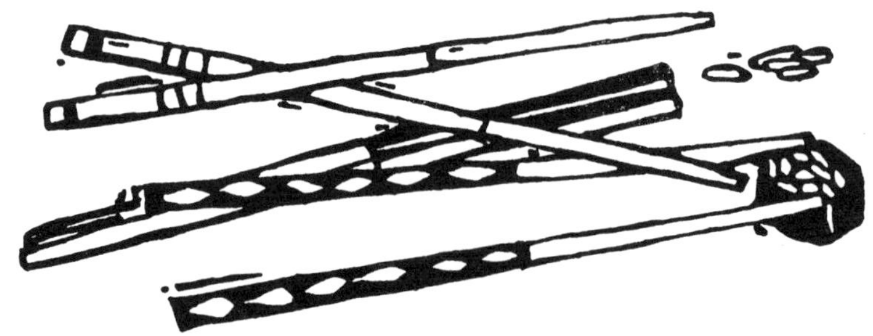

Muc Dua
(Dried Coconut Candy)

1 coconut
1 cup sugar
   water

Crack open the coconut and remove the milk. Scoop out the coconut meat from its shell, being careful to preserve the largest pieces you can. Then slice the meat into very thin strips. (A potato peeler works well.) Strips should be approximately 3″ long. Soak strips in water approximately 24 hours. After rinsing the strips in a colander, boil them in clear water for 20 minutes. Mix 1 cup of water with 1 cup of sugar. Pour that mixture and the coconut strips into a deep skillet over a medium heat. Stirring constantly, bring to a boil until the water is reduced by half. Next reduce the heat to low; continue stirring until the liquid vaporizes completely. Be careful that the strips do not burn. Keep stirring for another 30-60 seconds, even after the water has evaporated. If the strips begin to brown, remove immediately. Spread on a tray covered with aluminum foil. Then, using chopsticks or tongs, turn each strip individually until all are dry. (An easier way is to use two trays of equal size and flip the strips back and forth on them.) To add color, a few drops of food color can be added to the sugar/water mixture.

NOTE: Ma always makes huge batches of these treats, along with the gingerroot candy, to enjoy during the Tet. The bowls of red, blue and green muc dua always indicate that a celebration is at hand.

Muc Gung
(Gingerroot Candy)

To make gingerroot candy, follow the directions for Coconut Candy exactly, except that you add ½ teaspoon of salt to the water in which the pieces are soaked for 24 hours and the pieces cannot be sliced with a potato peeler. This candy, unlike the coconut candy, is never dyed with food coloring.

NOTE: Whenever I am hoarse or suffering from a sore throat, Ba prescribes a healthy dose of these very pungent candies. Though I much prefer the coconut candy, I dutifully eat this Vietnamese version of a throat lozenge. (It actually works for me!)

VII
"It Is As It Must Be"

Someone once said that to know a people, one had to experience both a wedding and a funeral, the two great cultural traditions. In retrospect, I have to agree.

I truly feel Vietnamese now. My "adopted" family had accepted me years earlier, I know; but it took the funeral of our beloved Ha, Lac's younger sister, to convince me that I am now *cung mot gra dinh*, one of them.

The Friday morning before Memorial Day we were awakened by a phone call, Lac's younger brother calling to ask if I could come over to help Ma. He added that Ha had fainted and was being taken to the hospital. "Sure thing," I replied, then thought—with more than a little irritation—of all the plans I had made for the day. Fainting is surely not uncommon among women, why all the fuss? Lac, who had scheduled one of his semiannual play days, had not left for work. He suggested that I call the hospital to check on Ha before we started across town.

He spoke with Ha's husband, Nhan, who said that she had just fallen over, that he had no word on her condition, that we should come directly to the hospital. He had already sent a friend to pick up Ma. After dropping the children off at school, we headed straight for the hospital. On the way, in the middle of aimless conversation, Lac declared, "You know, Paula. Women don't live long in my family,"—a reference to three sisters between him and Ha who had all died before their tenth birthday.

Even with Lac's premonition, I was unprepared for the shock of hearing that Ha was dead. Lac translated his mother's words, but I couldn't accept them. I was sure that there was an error in communication. After all, there had been so many times before. "No," I said, then again, "No . . . no . . . no," each time more loudly until Nga, Ha's five-month-old daughter, was screaming, terrified, with me. Lac guided me to a seat, then slumped down beside me. When I should have been trying to comfort Lac and Ma, when I should have reached out to console Nhan and his infant, I was battling instead with the simple act of breathing.

A nurse who had followed me into the prayer room nodded sympathetically. "Yes, she's dead, but she didn't suffer. We don't know what happened, but it was quick." Yes. Quick. A twenty-seven year old, perfectly healthy woman preparing for work one Friday morning falls over dead. Pfft! Just like that, one life gone, one world ended.

We waited in that cell-like room until all the family arrived for a private viewing of her body, the first of a series of Vietnamese funeral customs. Ma begged me to prevent the doctors from mutilating her body, and knowing that it was useless, I pled her case with the emergency room staff. "It is her wishes . . . please understand their culture . . . no autopsy . . . don't desecrate her body." Naturally, under the circumstances, no medical examiner would sign a death certificate without an autopsy. The body was delivered that afternoon to the County Medical Examiner's office.

The rest of the day we spent in seclusion, trying to explain Co Ha's death to our five and seven-year-old sons. "But we just ate dinner with Co Ha on Sunday, Mom. What happened to her? What about Nga? Mom, are you gonna die too?"

Nhan at first planned to have Ha's body cremated, in keeping with Buddhist tradition, but Ma begged him to reconsider. She wanted a grave to visit, to place incense on, and Nhan, of course, could not refuse. Knowing of only one funeral home, he selected Sun-

set Memorial Park and requested that Lac and I be there to clarify the plans. In anticipation of some strange requests, Lac and I arrived early to discuss traditions and culture with the director, a most understanding and patient man.

Accompanied by four other people including Ba and Ha's supervisor from work, Nhan arrived to plan the burial of his wife of eighteen months. Most of our requests were honored, whenever they fell within legal limits. He requested to burn candles at the head and foot of her casket, but fire marshall laws forbade that custom. He longed to sleep in the chapel with the body, as a loyal Vietnamese husband should. Again denied. No visitors may remain in the building after 9:00, a major disappointment for Nhan and the family, but non-negotiable.

Other requests were readily granted. Tables with food and beverages to feed the spirits could be maintained. Certainly, several of Ha's ceremonial dresses could be buried in the casket with her. Incense could burn, so long as mourners were present to tend the pots. And finally, the chanting of the ceremonies would not interfere with other services, for the chapel sat isolated from the remainder of the building.

The planning session dragged on longer than I had hoped, for all the details had to be discussed and argued among the committee who had nominated themselves. Even the time was debated, but 11:00 a.m. on Monday, Memorial Day was acceptable to everyone, since it would sidestep the need for time off from work. I argued for an obituary in the paper, a hangover from my "other life." That idea was summarily rejected, because, according to Ba, the Vietnamese community already knew of the loss of their "sister"—no need to print it. After four hours of planning, selecting caskets, flowers, and a burial site, as well as signing of papers, we left, feeling emotionally and physically drained.

But there was more to come that day. Much more.

We were required to be at the Trans' home to receive the mourners. Knowing that Vietnamese courtesy would extend even past the boundaries of death itself, Lac and I stopped and bought bushels of fried chicken, french fries, and cole slaw. By the time we arrived, however, the women of the community had converged. Food was not to be an issue for Ma to deal with for the next several days, though company was.

That evening Nhan and Ba set up an altar to Ha's spirit, which remains to this day. On it rests a large framed photograph of Ha, a pair of white candles, an incense burner, food and water, and Ha's makeup and sewing kits. Each day for three years the food must be replaced. And each spirit day, we must bow before her altar and burn incense to her spirit.

Sunday we had planned a quiet afternoon visit to the chapel to sit with Ha for a while, but that was not to be either. Arriving about noon, we landed in the midst of a crisis. The time of the ceremony had to be changed; it was essential that Ha's body be in the ground by 11:00, as declared by *thay phap*, a kind of Vietnamese fortune teller. If she went into the ground later, her spirit would not rest. I, as *Chi Hai*, was elected to change the plans—a more complicated task than usual. We had been told in painstaking detail during the planning session, that grave diggers do not work on holidays; we had to schedule them especially and pay overtime. Now, less than twenty-four hours from the burial, we were adamant about a time change.

After I discussed the issue with the director and stressed the importance to the family, he reluctantly made the arrangements. Now I was ready to go home, but Ba requested that we wait for the arrival of the monk from Houston. He was due about 6:00. Lac, angered by what he considered to be interference from outsiders, prepared to leave, but I reminded him that he is a part of the culture, and we were there to honor his sister. So we waited. And waited.

Presently a tall, bald Vietnamese man clad in saffron robes strode into the chapel, a paradox of commanding strength and quiet humility. Moving directly to the front of the chapel, he began the purification rites. First he approached the altar, praying and lighting incense. Next, chanting, he dipped a long-stemmed carnation into a cup of holy water and splashed it over the casket, the altar and the first few rows of mourners. Only then was he ready to begin the *cau xieu*, a prayer service for the forgiveness of Ha's sins.

After a lengthy prayer the monk moved to the casket, once again blessing it. On Ha's chest he laid an oblong piece of red paper with gold Chinese lettering. The purpose of this paper, *la bua*, is to guard Ha's spirit, so that evil spirits cannot claim it. It also frees her spirit from wandering aimlessly, becoming a "lost soul." According to Lac, this symbol is especially important for people who experience sudden, confusing deaths.

This rite completed, the monk motioned for Nhan to kneel before the altar for the blessing of the funeral robes. The immediate family of the deceased must wear heavy white gauze robes, a sign of mourning. As Nhan knelt, the monk placed the robe on him, tying it securely. Finally he wrapped a long white headband around Nhan's head. Nhan would traditionally wear this garb for three years of formal mourning, but to accommodate to American life, he now simply wears a small black or white patch on his shirt pocket. The baby Nga too was dressed in a miniature robe and headband—but by Ma, since a monk may never touch a female, not even a baby.

With these preliminaries behind us, the ceremony began in earnest. Praying and chanting and ringing of bells, incense burning and women wailing. I recall all of these images as vividly as if it occurred yesterday. What I remember most, though, concerns Nhan. I had never really cared much for him; in my opinion he was a typical macho Vietnamese male who used a gentle, loving woman to inflate his ego and serve him and his cronies. But that night I learned to respect him for his simple dignity, for his solemn endurance of an exhausting ritual. Throughout an hour of praying he continuously knelt, bowing three times whenever the monk rang his bell. His tribute to Ha— patient and compassionate—demonstrated a gentle side to his nature I had never before seen.

The next morning we were up at dawn to prepare for the burial service. Though we had decided not to allow our younger son to attend the funeral, Jason was given his choice. Through tears he said, "No,

Mom, I don't want to see Co Ha dead. But will you take her a rose for me?" We stopped at three different florist shops before we found pink roses, Ha's favorites. Placing them in the casket on her pillow, I wished her a peaceful journey and gave her the love of her nephews.

Then I observed a strange scene. A group of Vietnamese women approached the casket for their final farewell. At Ma's bidding, one attempted to take the wedding rings off of Ha's finger. They would not budge. Another tried, stopping just short of forcing the rings off. And then a third woman. She pulled and tugged, determined to remove the rings. Nothing happened. Ma signaled for Nhan, to whom she spoke quietly for several minutes. He stood before the casket, bowed three times, and whispered in her ear. When he reached for the rings, they slid off as easily as if her finger had been oiled. He had asked for her permission to take them, that they might be keepsakes for Nga.

The receiving line formed outside the chapel, and I took my place beside the *Anh Hai*. Uncomfortable as I was with that tradition, I served to greet the American mourners and thank them for their presence. I also collected the many envelopes for the family; the Vietnamese seldom send flowers but instead offer monetary gifts—usually substantial ones. During the three-day funeral, the community donated in excess of $7000 to help Nhan with expenses.

We waited for the monk's entrance, then filed in according to rank: Nhan and Nga wrapped in the white robes, Ma and Ba, Lac and me, Ha's younger brothers and sisters. The ceremony duplicated the one from the previous evening, all in Vietnamese, of course. Nhan again knelt and bowed, his strain beginning to show to careful observers. With his final bow to the altar, the monk signaled for eight young men, all dressed in white, to prepare the casket for final viewing and closure. As the mourners passed, a young woman handed them a flower from the bouquets surrounding the bier.

I did not pass again, for I had spoken my message in private earlier that morning. Instead, Co Lisa, a family friend, and I flanked Ma; her firm resolve was clearly dissolving as she watched the pallbearers closing the casket on this, her fourth daughter to die.

The procession formed according to tradition: A young Vietnamese man carrying a portrait of Ha led the way, followed by the pallbearers with the casket. Next was the monk, counting prayers on his prayer bracelet, and Nhan. A young man holding aloft a statue of the Buddha, then twelve beautiful young women bearing fruit and flowers. The family, and finally the remainder of the friends.

We gathered about the grave, Lisa and I forcing Ma to sit. An elder in the community grabbed a handful of the dirt and threw it in all four directions, invoking the spirits of the wind. The monk finished his prayer cycle, then lit many incense sticks and placed them in a gold pot. Setting the pot on the casket, he blessed the burial site. Next he placed burning incense at all four corners of the grave. Finally he put the food the young women had carried on the casket to be buried with Ha. With a final prayer, he signaled an end to the ceremony. The casket was lowered into the grave,

but no one moved. Each person awaited the ritual of the flowers. Nhan dropped his flowers first, then Ma, Ba, me, Lac; one by one, everyone dropped a flower onto the casket until it was totally covered by a blanket of crimson, gold and white. Still no movement. We watched as the gravediggers completed the burial, so that we could surround the grave with burning incense, a protection from evil.

While waiting for my turn to stick the incense in the ground, I noticed that a huge picnic banquet was being spread near the grave. After all these years as a Vietnamese, I don't know why I was surprised that there would be feasting after the funeral. Admittedly, few people actually feasted; nonetheless, food enough to feed several hundred people lay waiting.

We remained by the gravesite until all of the mourners had left. It was well past noon in the oppressive heat of a South Texas summer, yet there was no movement to leave. Lac finally said, "We can leave now, but Nhan must stay." I was appalled that he would be expected to sit on the grave in 96-degree weather; in Vietnam he would be expected to remain there for three full days. The image of that solitary figure sitting on a grave is etched in my mind.

We went home to rest and change clothes, before taking the boys over to the Trans' for a private ceremony at Ha's altar. Kneeling before the altar, Ba clasped three sticks of incense in his fists, prayed silently, then touched the incense to his forehead three times before bowing and placing it in a burner on the altar. Everyone else followed his pattern, until finally it was my turn. Unsure of myself, I looked to Lac, who nodded almost imperceptibly, so I knelt, prayed, and touched the incense to my head. Last of all, Nhan knelt before his wife's altar. Two hours later when we were preparing to leave, I found him still kneeling there, tears trickling down his cheek.

It was three full months before the coroner released his findings, but they came as no surprise to anyone in the family. I recounted the story of Ha's death to Dr. Bux, who listened attentively and respectfully. And the ruling was inevitable.

Ma has told us that Ha died because Huong came to claim her spirit. Huong was Ma's second daughter, the first having died at birth. Huong was born with a cleft lip that was to be repaired in an American army hospital when she was seven years old. The surgery went well, but the child was to remain overnight before dismissal. In the evening a fever attacked, and she was dead within a couple of hours. After a third daughter died mysteriously, Ma realized that the spirits did not want her to bear daughters.

Thus Ma made Huong her spirit guide. Whenever she lost an article, she prayed to Huong to help her find it. When she celebrated the Feasts of the Spirits, she always honored Huong. And she trained the children to respect her spirit guide as well. Although Ha never really knew her sister, she grew up loving her as Ma did.

Though educated in the United States, Ha's major goal in life was to be a Vietnamese wife, to bear many children, in brief, to live the life her mother has lived. So three months after her marriage, she was delighted to announce that Chi Hai was to become Co Paula. My niece was born on Christmas Eve. Two months later Huong appeared to Ha in a dream and announced, "Now that Nga is here, it is time for you to come with me." This dream frightened Ha so much that she refused to play in the water at the beach for fear that Huong would pull her down. And two months later Ha literally dropped dead.

Dr. Bux searched and searched; then to satisfy his scientific curiosity, he consulted other specialists. They all agreed: no apparent cause for death. In giving up, Dr. Bux released a death certificate that states simply, "Cause of Death: Undetermined." I suppose he couldn't rule, "Huong Came For Her."

Now, months later I find myself frequently standing over Nga's crib as the toddler sleeps, a ragged bear clutched in tiny fists, a dark tendril curled about an angelic face. Watching her, this tiny image of her mother, I feel Ha's presence, the gentleness of her spirit. I recall Ha's typically Vietnamese response to my expression of concern over her "hasty pregnancy," especially in view of serious financial difficulties. With a slight shrug, "It is as it must be." Ha must have known what I could never have foreseen, and, in dying, she left us all the gift of life.

Glossary of Ingredients

Since you may be unfamiliar with many of the ingredients common in Vietnamese kitchens (as I once was), I am including this brief listing and some suggested substitutes. Many of these items may be found in the gourmet sections of American markets; the rest are available in Oriental markets.

ALSA—A baking additive made in France, composed primarily of baking powder and corn starch. Substitute: 2 teaspoons of baking powder and ½ teaspoon corn starch for one packet of Alsa.

BAMBOO SHOOTS—Fresh bamboo or sun dried shoots are commonly used in Vietnamese recipes. Since these are often unavailable, you may substitute canned Chinese bamboo sprouts. Many health food stores are now stocking dried bamboo shoots; however, they are oven dried and must be soaked for 10-15 minutes before use.

BANANA LEAVES—The leaves from ordinary banana plants are used for wrapping foods to be steamed. They are usually tied with a heavy string. Substitutes: aluminum foil bound and tied tightly (but you will need to add extra time for the steaming process), or clean cotton cloths, such as tea-towels.

BEAN CURD—A curd with a cheese-like texture which is made from soybean. May be bought in supermarkets in the refrigerated foods section. The hard bean curd is easier to prepare. There is also a soft, smoother variety. Bean curd or tofu is a high protein, cholesterol-free food.

BEAN SAUCE—A strong, spicy brown sauce which comes in hot and mild selections. These are available only in Oriental markets; our favorites are Mijako and Szechuen brands.

BEAN SPROUTS—Tender shoots of the mung bean. The Vietnamese use these crunchy sprouts to enhance the flavor of many soups and in most stir-fried vegetable dishes.

BEAN THREADS—Often called cellophane noodles for their translucent quality. Made from mung beans, the vermicelli-like noodles must be soaked in water before using.

CABBAGE, CHINESE—Commonly called *bok choy*, this is a leafy cabbage, with long, crinkle-edged leaves. Regular cabbage may be substituted but the flavor will be stronger and different.

CABBAGE, PRESERVED—Chinese cabbage that has been soaked in vinegar and salt for three to four days. This cabbage is similar to the Korean *kim chee*, which involves the fermentation of several varieties of vegetables with peppers.

CHAR SIU MIXTURE—A red, powder-like barbeque mixture used to coat pork, chicken, or duck. Now it is available in bottles, but these contain high levels of sugar, which do not appeal to the Vietnamese palate.

CILANTRO—Pungent leaves of fresh coriander (sometimes called Chinese parsley). Cilantro is similar to Italian flat-leaf parsley, but more rounded in shape. (Any substitution of another parsley changes the flavor radically.)

CITRONELLA ROOT—Commonly known as lemongrass, citronella is a grass-like plant that grows wild in tropical climates. The lower part of the stem is the edible portion; it carries a pungent, delightful odor. There is a powdered form of lemongrass. Other, less satisfactory, substitutes include grated fresh lemon peel or thin slices of fresh gingerroot. (If the word "lemongrass" is part of the title of the recipe, such as "Chicken Lemongrass," the *real* thing is the only thing!)

COCONUT MILK—This is NOT the watery substance in the middle of a coconut. It is make by blending the coconut meat with a roughly equal measure of warm water—on low for one minute, then on high for two to three minutes. Strain through a cloth and refrigerate. It is also available in cans. Substitute: one tablespoon heavy cream for ¼ cup of coconut milk.

DAIKON—A long, white radish available in specialty stores.

FISH SAUCE (Nuoc Mam)—A clear, brown sauce made in barrels containing fresh fish alternated with layers of salt. After fermentation, the sauce is drained off, purified, and bottled. There is no substitute!

GINGERROOT—Odd-shaped root of a tropical Asian plant. The fresh root is preferable to the powdered variety, which may be substituted. A better choice is dried gingerroot, commonly available in health food stores; but it must be soaked in warm water for several hours.

HOISIN SAUCE—A sweet brown sauce, much thicker in consistency than soy sauce or fish sauce.

LEMONGRASS—See CITRONELLA ROOT.

MAGGI SEASONING—A high grade of soy sauce bottled in Switzerland, of all places! Lac claims that all other soy sauces are made for cooking; Maggi goes directly onto the sandwiches, soups, etc., before eating.

MONOSODIUM GLUTAMATE (MSG)—The Vietnamese use this flavor enhancer sparingly. It may be eliminated with little effect.

MUNG BEANS—Used to grow bean sprouts. Dried mung beans that have been hulled are yellowish and are often used as fillings for stuffed cakes and as additions to sweet rice.

MUSHROOMS, BLACK—These dried mushrooms have a meaty, smoky flavor, and a chewy texture. They must be soaked in hot water before use; the hard stems are to be discarded. Fresh large mushrooms may be substituted with little loss of flavor.

NOODLES—Vietnamese noodles are frequently made of rice and range in textures from vermicelli to ¼ inch ribbons. They are usually dried and must be cooked, but since they are rice, the cooking time is much shorter than that of the wheat varieties. The latter may serve as substitutions, but with a considerably different taste.

OYSTER SAUCE—A strong, rich sauce made of soy sauce and oysters.

POTATO STARCH—An agent used to thicken sauces and to bind meat to form meatballs. Substitutes: tapioca, corn, or rice starch.

RICE PAPER—A very popular Vietnamese food, used in many dishes. It must be dampened to soften for wrapping. It has little taste of its own.

SERRANO PEPPERS—One of many varieties of chili peppers. They are quite hot, and served in one form or another at almost every Vietnamese meal. May substitute other peppers to taste.

SHRIMP, DRIED—These are tiny shrimp that are oven dried, producing a strong flavor, which some find too powerful. Before use, they should be soaked in warm water for ten minutes.

SHRIMP PASTE—Dried shrimp which has been ground up and moistened. Should be used sparingly, as the flavor is intense.

SOY SAUCE—A dark brown sauce made from soybean, used to flavor most Chinese dishes. Vietnamese cooks rely more heavily on the fish sauce.

SWEET RICE—A full-bodied, long-grain rice with an off-white to yellowish coloring. It is usually soaked for several hours before cooking and is a mainstay of the Vietnamese peasant diet. Oriental markets are the only places I have ever found this product, but like all rices, it will last indefinitely if stored in air-tight containers.

STAR ANISE SEED—A strong spice shaped like a star, commonly used in Vietnamese soups. When cooking, it smells strongly of licorice.

TOFU—See BEAN CURD.

WATER CHESTNUTS—A very crisp root vegetable with a slightly sweet flavor. They are frequently used in stir-fried vegetable dishes. Fresh chestnuts must be peeled, while canned ones may be used right from the can.

WHITE RADISH—A root-like member of the radish family that has large white bulbs. This vegetable is used to spice up a salad or it can be pickled.

WONTON WRAPPERS—Small, flat pieces of pastry, approximately two inches square. These are stuffed with meats and either fried or cooked in soup. They are now commonly sold in the refrigerated section of supermarkets.

INDEX OF RECIPES